BACH FLOWER

REMEDIES

BACH FLOWER
REMEDIES

Stefan Ball

TEACH YOURSELF BOOKS

For UK orders: please contact Bookpoint Ltd, 39 Milton Park, Abingdon, Oxon OX14 4TD. Telephone: (44) 01235 400414, Fax: (44) 01235 400454. Lines are open from 9.00–6.00, Monday to Saturday, with a 24-hour message answering service. Email address: orders@bookpoint.co.uk

For USA & Canada orders: please contact NTC/Contemporary Publishing, 4255 West Touhy Avenue, Lincolnwood, Illinois 60646–1975, USA. Telephone: (847) 679 5500, Fax: (847) 679 2494.

Long renowned as the authoritative source for self-guided learning – with more than 30 million copies sold worldwide – the *Teach Yourself* series includes over 200 titles in the fields of languages, crafts, hobbies, business and education.

British Library Cataloguing in Publication Data
A catalogue record for this title is available from The British Library.

Library of Congress Catalog Card Number: On file

First published in UK 2000 by Hodder Headline Plc, 338 Euston Road, London, NW1 3BH.

First published in US 2000 by NTC/Contemporary Publishing, 4255 West Touhy Avenue, Lincolnwood (Chicago), Illinois 60646–1975 USA.

The 'Teach Yourself' name and logo are registered trade marks of Hodder & Stoughton Ltd.

Cover photo from Barbara Bellingham
Illustrations by Jane Taylor
Typeset by Transet Limited, Coventry, England.
Printed in Great Britain for Hodder & Stoughton Educational, a division of Hodder Headline Plc, 338 Euston Road, London NW1 3BH by Cox & Wyman Ltd, Reading, Berkshire.

Impression number   10 9 8 7 6 5 4 3 2 1
Year   2006 2005 2004 2003 2002 2001 2000

CONTENTS

ACKNOWLEDGEMENTS

Bach practitioners Tony Hobbs and Pamela Higginson allowed me to include case studies of theirs, my wife Chris read parts of the manuscript, and Loulou Brown suggested improvements. My thanks to them, and to everyone else who has influenced the contents in any way.

ABOUT THIS BOOK

I had two objectives in planning and writing this book. The first was to be true to the title, and to the aims of the *Teach Yourself* series. With this in mind I have written activities, questions and exercises into the text. You can read through the book at one sitting, using it as a straightforward introduction, but if you work through the exercises you will be able to be your own teacher, as the title promises.

The second objective was to define what readers of books like this want, and to meet that need. I have made a number of assumptions: that you are a beginner, not a specialist – perhaps someone who has not used the remedies at all, or someone who has never progressed beyond the occasional use of Rescue Remedy; that you want knowledge that can be used to improve your life; and that you want to make practical use of the remedies.

The book falls into three main sections.

- Chapters 1 and 2 provide basic information. You will learn how to select and take remedies, and about the benefits of using them. I also look at the history of the remedies and at the current state of research into their properties.
- In chapters 3 to 10 you will learn what the individual remedies are for, so that you will know when to select them.
- Chapters 11 and 12 build on the knowledge you have gained, first by suggesting ways in which you can move beyond self-help, and second by troubleshooting some of the trickier questions about remedy use.

At the end of the book there is a glossary where you can look up remedies and technical terms as you work through the main text, followed by a repertory of key words that will help if you are unsure where to start looking for a particular emotion.

The standard method of describing what the remedies are for is to give *indications* – for instance, 'Gentian is the remedy for those who feel despondent.' As well as indications, this book provides examples of remedies in action and tells you what the result of taking the correct remedy would be. So, you will read about 46-year-old Hannah and her efforts to return to work, and about the way she feels after taking Gentian. I believe that presenting remedies in action makes them more relevant to real life. It also, I hope, makes learning the indications more interesting.

Other books written about Bach Flower Remedies tend to adopt one of two possible solutions to the problem of presenting all 38 remedies. The first is to list them alphabetically. The second is to group them under the seven headings that Dr Bach used in his description of the remedies (Remedies for Fear, Remedies for Loneliness etc.). The alphabetical method has the advantage of making it easy to look up a remedy – but the order is arbitrary, which makes it difficult to highlight similarities and differences between similar remedies. Using Dr Bach's own groupings solves this problem in part, but many beginners say that they find the rationale behind the groups difficult to understand.

Bearing these problems in mind, I have presented the remedies in chapters 4 to 9 under loose headings such as 'Fear and Worry', 'Depression and Hope' and 'When Something Happens'. These are not alternative groupings to Dr Bach's, but an educational convenience. Because they are informal, ad hoc groups, I can list the same remedy under more than one heading, which not only points up differences and relationships more effectively, but also gives you the opportunity to recap on remedies as you work through the text.

Dr Bach's great wish was that everyone should have access to his work. My hope is that this book will help in a small way to make that wish come true.

1 INTRODUCING BACH FLOWER REMEDIES

Aims of this chapter

This chapter answers the questions that people often ask when they come across Bach Flower Remedies for the first time.

■ What are Bach Flower Remedies?
■ What do they do?
■ What is in them?
■ How do I use them?
■ Do they work? – and if so, how do they work?

Holistic theories of health

The *Shorter Oxford Dictionary* defines holism as 'the theory or principle of a tendency in nature to form or produce organized wholes which are more than the mere sum of the component units', and in particular 'the application of this theory in medicine, involving the treatment of the whole person rather than the physical symptoms alone.' Holism says that everything in your life is linked. Your job security, your family relationships, spiritual beliefs and hobbies, the clothes you wear, the exercise you take, and the way you feel about yourself and your life are all relevant to your health. There is no sense in isolating one aspect and treating that alone. Sensible physicians look at the whole person.

Looking at the whole person is not a new idea in medicine. We can find it in the *Hippocratic Collection*, a series of treatises on health and medical ethics and the source of the Hippocratic oath sworn by doctors when they graduate. These writings date from before 375 BC. Their author, the Greek physician Hippocrates, taught that patients should be seen as a whole, and that doctors should spend time looking at people rather than diseases.

Holism sounds like simple common sense but for most of the twentieth century doctors studied disease symptoms and ignored the emotional and spiritual needs of their patients. Even today administrative and academic arrangements, such as the organization of hospitals into departments based on different parts of the body, continue to reinforce the mechanical view of people as sets of divisible parts. Nevertheless, attitudes have changed a lot over the last 20 or 30 years. Most doctors try to support their patients on more than one level, and you will hear holism and empowerment mentioned in the most orthodox circles.

Medicine for the emotions

Even in holistic practice, most medicines treat physical problems. Drugs may control severe emotional disturbances, but attempts to 'cure' mental states like anxiety, worry and lack of confidence usually take on different and less material forms: psychoanalysis, psychotherapy, counselling and so on. This is what makes Bach Flower Remedies such an unusual proposition. Put simply, Bach Flower Remedies are medicines for the emotions. Each remedy treats a specific negative emotional state by encouraging the corresponding positive quality that lies dormant within us. People who feel despondent take an encouragement remedy in order to leave the negative state behind. Others who feel anxious take a remedy that brings out their natural reserves of courage.

As their name suggests, most Bach Flower Remedies come from the flowering parts of plants and bushes and trees. There are two methods of production. In the first, flowers are floated on water and left in full sunlight. The warmth of the sun imprints the healing quality of the flower into the water, in a process similar to homeopathic potentisation. In the second, flowering twigs are boiled to transfer their healing quality to the water. Whichever method is used, the energized water is mixed with alcohol so as to preserve it and the resulting liquid, called *mother tincture*, is diluted at a ratio of two drops to 30 mls of brandy in order to make *stock remedies*. This is the strength you can buy in the shops. Every 10 ml bottle contains two-thirds of a drop of mother tincture; the rest is brandy. There are no added ingredients beyond the plant, water and brandy.

The remedies come as a liquid so that you can mix them together. There are only 38 in the system – not many compared to the thousands of homeopathic medicines, or the millions of orthodox drugs in the pharmacy – but mixing them gives nearly 293 million possible combinations, enough to treat every possible negative mental state.

Using the remedies is so simple that the basics can be given in a few words. Start by thinking about your situation and how you feel about it. Then try to isolate the emotional elements that make up your overall mental state. If you feel fed up, what exactly does 'fed up' feel like to you? Does it mean you feel sorry for yourself? Does it mean that you become irritable with the people around you? Does it mean that you withdraw into your shell and avoid seeing friends? In some cases you will identify one single emotion, and then you can take the one remedy that resolves that feeling. More often you will find a mix of feelings, for example when you are fed up you may feel sorry for yourself, *and* irritable, *and* inclined to withdraw, all at the same time. In this case you take a mixture of remedies to address the specific emotions you have identified.

We will look at selection and dosage in more detail further on in this book.

Dr Edward Bach

The 38 remedies were the life's work of Edward Bach, a highly respected Harley Street doctor, pathologist and bacteriologist. Dr Bach grew dissatisfied with orthodox medicine and its concentration on isolated symptoms. He came to believe that unhappiness and fear led to ill-health, and that true healing meant arresting disease at its emotional source, before the physical symptoms appeared. With this in mind he sought a direct way of treating the whole person by way of the emotions.

Dr Bach studied homeopathy when he worked at the London Homeopathic Hospital. From that system he borrowed the idea of type or constitutional remedies – in other words, remedies that treat the personality – and the idea of preparing minute doses of a substance. Another influence was his own brush with death, which took place when he haemorrhaged and collapsed in July 1917. He was rushed into an operating theatre, where surgeons removed a cancerous growth. When he came round they told him he had a matter of months to live – but his commitment to his research led him back to his laboratory as soon as he could walk. As time passed he became stronger, much to everybody's surprise, and this experience strengthened his belief in the power of mind and emotion over illness. He had got better because he had a purpose in life and was determined to see it through. If other sick people could rediscover their sense of purpose they might be able to do the same.

Much of Dr Bach's early research concerned the problem of chronic disease. He isolated seven types of bacteria that were found in vastly increased numbers in people suffering from chronic disease, and used them to prepare vaccines. These proved to be powerful medicines in the treatment of chronic bowel conditions. In his period at the London Homeopathic Hospital he prepared the bacteria using homeopathic methods, which meant that he was able to give them by mouth and so avoid the use of painful injections. The next step was to replace the bacteria with plants. He believed that medicine should be as pure and natural as possible, and using plants would be a welcome move towards greater simplicity.

The discovery of the flower remedies took seven years. Dr Bach found the first three plants in 1928. At first he prepared them in a laboratory using homeopathic methods, just as he had prepared bacteria in the past, and he used them to treat the same group of chronic diseases. But it soon became apparent that the new remedies were different. The bacterial remedies treated bowel disease, but the new flower remedies worked directly on the emotions. They could help far more people, including those with very different physical symptoms and diseases.

By 1930 Dr Bach was so excited at the direction his research was taking him that he left London and a yearly income of £5,000 to devote himself full-time to the search for new flower remedies. He walked all over southern Britain, from Wales to the Norfolk coast, before settling down in a cottage near Wallingford, Oxfordshire, in 1934. Along the way he discovered a further 35 remedies – the last

19 in the countryside around his new home – and the special methods of preparation that are so characteristic of his work.

Bach died a year after announcing that he had completed his work. He was 50 years old, and had outlived the diagnosis of his medical friends by 18 years. Since then the remedies have spread all over the world. Millions of people use them to help themselves, or take them under the guidance of therapists and practitioners. Orthodox medical practitioners value them, and the former New York City Commissioner of Mental Health, J Herbert Fill, used Bach Flower Remedies in his psychiatric practice, preferring them to tranquillizers because of the absence of side-effects. Nurses in Britain and the US can study Bach Flower Remedies on officially accredited courses. In the UK and Italy students can attend university courses on the remedies. This growing professional and academic respectability contrasts with the fate of many of the experimental techniques of the 1930s, which died along with their founders.

The effects of emotional dis-ease

Dr Bach believed that the body has its own natural state of health. Illness is an unnatural state, and in order to become ill something must happen to knock the body out of balance.

In the classic scientific view the something that happens is infection by a virus or a bacteria, or an allergic reaction. The agent of disease starts off out there in the environment. We erect barriers against it by building better drains and arranging vaccination programmes. But sometimes the enemy gets through and invades the body. When this happens the body has to fight. Medicine helps by attacking the invader with drugs, and at the same time it declares martial law, suppressing fevers, vomiting, diarrhoea and runny noses. It pacifies both body and disease, while the more mechanical medical arts – the engineering corps in this war for health – mend fractures and patch wounds.

There is some truth in the military view of disease, but it is not the whole truth. Looking at illness and the people who became ill Dr Bach asked why it was that two similar people could be exposed to the same external cause of a disease but only one of them become ill. We all know this to be true from our everyday lives. Some people never catch a cold, while others sneeze all year round. Explanations such as 'so-and-so has a weaker immune system' do not answer the question *why* some people's immune systems are weaker than others.

Dr Bach considered the possibility that there could be something about people's personalities and emotions that attracted illness or wellness. He noticed that people who lived fulfilling lives got sick less often than their unhappy and frustrated neighbours. Their everyday levels of health seemed to be pitched higher. They felt well in themselves, and when they did become sick – as he himself had done – they recovered faster and more completely. Emotional balance seemed to have a positive effect on physical health and emotional imbalance had a negative effect. Bach found wisdom in the words used to describe the approach of illness, as he explained during a lecture in 1936:

> Little Tommy comes home from school unusually tired, or drowsy, or irritable, or wanting to be fussed, or perhaps left alone and so on. He is 'not quite himself' as we say. Kind neighbours come in and say, 'Tommy is sickening for something, you will have to wait.' But why wait? If Tommy is treated then according to his mood, he may very soon again be turned from 'not quite himself' into 'quite himself', when whatever illness was threatened will not occur.

When Dr Bach was alive most professionals would have dismissed these ideas as cranky. Even people who believed in the importance of happiness did not have a model to explain how it could affect health. Today, however, all healthcare workers accept that the majority of illnesses – including AIDS, allergies, alopecia, angina, asthma, cancer, diabetes, dyspepsia, heart attacks, hypertension, irritable bowel syndrome, migraine, peptic ulcer, pre-menstrual tension, rheumatoid arthritis, skin diseases and tinnitus – are stress-related, and that happy people tend to live longer and more healthy lives. And a whole branch of medical research has been set up to investigate the biological links between emotional health and the immune system. The name of this new science is psychoneuroimmunology (PNI) –

it was born in the USA during the 1970s and 1980s and over the last decade it has spread to Europe and the rest of the world.

Psychoneuroimmunology has shown a clear relationship between the activity of the immune system and that of the nervous system. One study found that depressed middle-aged men were more likely to develop cancer, another that people who described themselves as without hope were more likely to die, and a third that people with cancer had suffered disproportionately from depression and unhappy childhoods. The physical links between emotions and the immune system turn out to be a group of chemical messengers called cytokinins. Cytokinins exist in both the bloodstream and spinal fluid. The way you feel – your emotional state – controls the type of cytokinins that your body produces, and so affects the immune system. When you feel depressed your nervous system produces a particular type of cytokinin that inhibits immune cell receptors. If you are under a lot of stress, however, stimulatory cytokinins are produced, and these over-stimulate the immune system. In both cases the out-of-balance emotions lead to negative effects on the immune system: either it is suppressed or it is over-active to the point of collapse.

Psychoneuroimmunology has given academic respectability to the beliefs of Dr Bach and other holistic practitioners, and has led to a shift in medical language. In their book *Mindwatching*, the well-known psychologists Hans and Michael Eysenck review the proven links between dysfunctional personalities and serious diseases such as cancer and coronary heart diseases. 'We simply have to give up the notion of body as opposed to mind,' they say, 'and accept the notion of a body-mind-soul entity.' Holism has always taken it as an article of faith that mind, body and spirit are linked. Now for the first time the linking mechanism has been found.

Bach Flower Remedies in everyday life

We can wait until we feel ill and then use the remedies. They will help us get our emotions back into a positive balance and this in turn lets our bodies return to their natural state of health. But as Dr Bach said, why wait?

Dr Bach did not see the remedies as traditional medicines, to be used only as directed, but as natural resources like air, water and food, that people can call on whenever they need to. His colleague and biographer Nora Weeks remembered him saying that taking a remedy should be as simple and obvious as eating a lettuce when we are hungry. This means that the remedies can become part of our everyday lives. We can take them at work and at home, when we are travelling and when we are standing still. Every time we feel under pressure or unhappy there is a remedy to bring us back to ourselves. This preventative use of the remedies helps us stay in balance so that disease is less likely to strike.

Research

Nobody knows exactly how the remedies work. In Dr Bach's time people talked about vibrations, and he would have been very interested in the ultrasound machines used by modern clinicians to see inside the human body. These work on the principle that different parts of the body vibrate at different pitches, and that sound waves can alter these bodily vibrations. Perhaps the remedies work in the same kind of way, each one relating to the different vibration rate of a particular emotion.

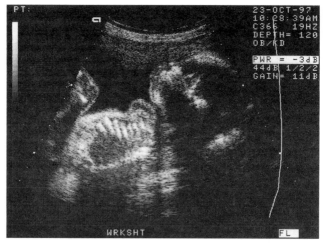

Figure 1.1 Ultrasound machines work because our bodies vibrate at different pitches

Nowadays the preferred description of the remedies' active ingredient is that it is a 'subtle energy'. Evidence for this includes some intriguing Kirlian photographs, published in Germany, that seem to show different characteristic patterns associated with different remedies. But Kirlian photography, which involves passing electric currents through an object placed on a photographic plate in order to record the resulting corona, has its detractors. Sceptics don't take it seriously as a scientific process. And until somebody does establish an accepted way of measuring emotional vibrations and subtle energies the forces involved will remain theoretical concepts, little more than metaphors for something that we don't understand.

The lack of a measuring device, along with the lack of clinical research into the remedies, has led to accusations that they are just placebos, and that their only effect is to give people the illusion of control. Defenders of Dr Bach's work could point to the way people use remedies to help animals and young babies, both groups largely immune to the power of suggestion. But the overriding argument that the remedies are more than placebos is that they consistently do what they claim to do, even when people don't know they are taking them. The remedies have helped countless millions since they were discovered 70 years ago. And the few small-scale studies that researchers have carried out have tended to show positive results.

In 1979 the Californian researcher Michael Weisglas wrote his doctoral thesis on Bach Flower Remedies, under the title *Personal Growth And Conscious Evolution Through Bach Flower Essences*. Weisglas carried out a double-blind study over a period of six weeks. He assigned 31 people at random to one of three groups, one taking mixes of four remedies, one mixes of seven, and one taking a placebo that did not contain any remedies. He tested the emotional states of his subjects before, during and at the end of the six-week period by using the Lüscher Colour Test, which involves ranking colours in order of preference, and a check list questionnaire containing 300 emotional and mental adjectives.

Weisglas found that the group of people taking a mix of four remedies showed a significantly higher degree of self-acceptance and understanding as compared with the placebo group. The group of people taking seven remedies, however, did not do as well, leading Weisglas to suggest that this number of remedies should only be used in extreme situations, as they seemed to set up interference patterns between them.

We could make a number of criticisms of this study. The Lüscher Colour Test is generally out of favour as a reliable measure of emotion. The small number of people in the sample groups casts doubt on how far its results could be extrapolated to the wider community. We could also criticize Weisglas' methods of selecting remedies, and the fact that he assigned subjects at random to a group that was obliged to take seven remedies. This is the maximum number of remedies normally recommended, and most of the time people take mixes of three, four or five. It is likely then that people in this group took a number of remedies that they did not need, and this would indeed interfere with the efficient working of the others.

Much of the more recent scientific research on the remedies has been carried out in Italy, where medical doctors have shown a great deal of interest in the remedies. At a conference in Milan in 1999 a number of papers were presented that seemed to show objective proof that the remedies work. Paediatrician Dr S Calzolari spent three years studying 417 children aged between 0 and 14 years, and found that the remedies were very effective in dealing with their emotional problems. Her results also gave objective proof of something that has been remarked on many times, namely the fact that the remedies work especially quickly with younger children and babies.

Another study carried out by Drs D'Auria and Pezza showed the usefulness of Bach Flower Remedies in the control of the psychological components of pain. A third, carried out by Drs Rossi and Setti, showed the action of particular remedies on crystalline substances called phyllosilicates. Rossi and Setti claimed that their unusual approach to evaluating the action of the remedies proved conclusively that the remedies are indeed active substances, each one with its own effects – despite the fact that conventional chemical analysis of remedies shows them to contain nothing but brandy and water. 'Having definitively proved the active potential of Bach Flowers,' they concluded, 'the only thing left to do is move on to the level of clinical demonstration, and pass from the level of the sensitive, crystalline and inorganic to that of the sensitive, organic and living.' (*La Medicina Biologica*, anno XVII, supplemento al no. 2 Aprile-Giugno 1999 – the translation is the author's.)

Until someone mounts a full-scale clinical trial at the organic, living level of human beings the level of proof will not be enough to convince determined sceptics. There are moves being made in this area, after many false starts, and a trial looking at the use of Rescue Remedy in UK dental practice is planned for early in the twenty-first century. Fortunately there is no need to wait for that, and we can all carry out our own trials of the claims made for the remedies by taking them when we need them. It is as simple as eating lettuce, as Dr Bach might have said.

Recap

- Flower Remedies are medicines used to balance negative mental states and emotions.
- They were discovered between 1928 and 1935 by a well-respected Harley Street doctor and homeopath, Dr Edward Bach.
- Dr Bach believed that the ultimate cause of disease was a lack of inner harmony, and that by resolving this disharmony health would come back naturally.
- Recent research in the field of psychoneuroimmunology supports the views of Dr Bach and others like him, that emotions have a decisive impact on physical health.
- Nobody can say how Bach Flower Remedies work, but they have proved themselves over time. The few studies that have been done have shown good results.

2 | USING BACH FLOWER REMEDIES

Aims of this chapter

This chapter covers the mechanics of using the 38 remedies.

- How to select remedies for the way you feel.
- How to select remedies for your personality.
- How to mix and take remedies.
- When and how to change the mix of remedies you are taking.

Selecting for day-to-day problems

The most straightforward way to use the remedies is as a way of getting out of a negative mood. Imagine you go to the office early in the morning. You have a lot of work to do, but find it difficult to get started. Instead of writing the urgent report you have on your desk you shuffle your in-tray about, or read non-urgent emails about the Christmas party. The remedy for this state of mind is Hornbeam. All you need to do is take Hornbeam until the feeling has passed.

We call remedies used like this *mood remedies*. A mood remedy is any remedy you take to get you over a bad mood. We can use all of the 38 remedies as mood remedies, and in the course of a lifetime all of us will experience all 38 of the basic moods.

Day-to-day selection involves being aware of how we feel and mapping those feelings to remedies. Psychologists call a self-aware consciousness of one's emotions a *metamood*. Metamood is possible because our minds are not unified blocks but subtle combinations of mental processes. Think of your emotional self as the driver in a car – metamood is the examiner in the passenger seat, able to think about your emotions instead of thinking with them.

Most of the time we can easily achieve metamood, and the more attention we give to our feelings the easier it is for us to understand and express them. But sometimes things get in the way. We may find our thoughts disturbing or unattractive, and deliberately or unconsciously refuse to acknowledge them. We may be so caught up in a state of mind that it controls every part of us – we can't say how we feel because we can't be objective – or be so out of tune with our emotions that we barely notice them, and find it hard to say whether anxiety or depression or anger is responsible for our unhappiness. Fortunately we can learn to recognize what our moods feel and look like even if metamood does not come naturally to us.

In some cases achieving metamood may be enough by itself to help us overcome negative emotions. If you know that you feel angry you might be able to choose to feel something else, such as tolerance, patience or forbearance instead. But if you do not have this level of control over your emotions (and most of us don't, most of the time) then the remedies can help.

EXERCISES
Mood remedies and metamood

These exercises can help you define how you feel, and get you into the habit of thinking about emotions.

A Try to think of a time you were frightened. What frightened you? How did you express your fear, and how did you try to cope with it? (You can repeat this exercise with other emotions instead of fear.)

B Look through any book, magazine or newspaper that contains photographs of real people in real situations. Try to define the mood each person is in. What are you basing your guesses on?

C Sit in front of a mirror. Think about something that scares you and note how your face looks when you are afraid. Look for the shape of your mouth, where your eyebrows are and what your eyes do. Now think about something that makes you angry. What does this look like? Repeat for different emotions.

D Think about a bad time you went through in the past. What emotions were you feeling? How could changing the way you felt have helped deal with that bad time?

E Pick a day in the next week when you expect to be under stress. On that day, make a special effort to keep track of how you feel hour by hour. At the end of the day try to answer the following questions: What provoked each feeling? Did you display your feelings, and if so how? Were the actions you took that day based more on your feelings or more on reasoned thought? Were the apparent feelings masks for something else? Was there one overriding emotion that could sum up the way you felt that day? Finally, what was the best, most constructive and most positive emotion you went through?

Other selection methods

In the years since Dr Bach's death people have tried to come up with ways of selecting remedies that would avoid the need for metamood. The approaches taken include filling in questionnaires, muscle-testing and dowsing. None of them has proved satisfactory, but we will review them here for the sake of completeness.

Questionnaires

Questionnaires have a long and very respectable history in psychological research, where they have proved successful in measuring clearly defined personality traits such as introversion, extroversion and psychotic tendencies. In contrast, remedy questionnaires attempt to evaluate a wide range of mental states made up of deep-seated characteristics and a mix of more temporary moods. The simpler versions offer lists of yes/no questions, with one, two or three questions for each remedy. A typical question would be 'I feel frightened of something I can name – YES/NO'. At the end of the questionnaire you add up the scores and take the seven or so remedies with the most number of 'Yes' answers. More complex questionnaires may contain hundreds of words describing mental states – hate, love and all points between. Again, you select those words which most strongly apply to the way you feel, and simple addition leads to a list of remedies.

Questionnaires might seem a quick and easy option at first, and they can be effective up to a point. The drawback is that people using questionnaires have no incentive to think deeply about how they feel. They tend not to learn the remedies and end up as consumers, using remedies like magic bullets, and trying to zap their negative feelings instead of understanding them in relation to their lives. This to my mind is a denial of the holistic principle. The difference between thinking for yourself and using a questionnaire is the difference between painting and painting-by-numbers. When you use a questionnaire, someone else has drawn in the lines.

Having said that, questionnaires do at least require us to give some thought to how we feel. So-called mechanical and intuitive approaches have gone further, and removed any need for self-awareness.

Muscle-testing

One of the best known of the mechanical approaches is kinesiology. Kinesiology means the study of bodily motion, but in complementary health it refers to a technique that seeks to discover and rectify energy flows in muscles. To diagnose for sensitivity to a particular food – or a particular remedy – practitioners place it in contact with the client and use their hands to test the strength of a muscle related to the contact area. Hence the other name for this technique, muscle-testing.

Dowsing and intuition

A similar approach is to use dowsing. Traditional dowsing involves looking for underground water or lost objects using a specially cut stick, but people dowsing for remedies use a pendulum, a weight of some kind suspended on string. They hold the pendulum over each bottle in turn, and choose those that cause the pendulum to oscillate in a particular way. Purely intuitive methods include touching bottles and choosing those that feel especially warm or cold, selecting remedies based on your emotional response to pictures of the remedy flowers, and picking out bottles at random.

There is a place for intuition in selecting remedies, although it should be a partner to self-awareness and not a replacement for it. Unfortunately techniques like these amount to an abdication of responsibility. If the pendulum tells us we need Vervain we may have no idea why, and may not even recognize that we have any symptoms requiring Vervain in us. This leaves us in the same position as any other helpless patient, waiting for someone or something to point us to an unintelligible cure. In the end the long way round is the simplest. The best way to use the remedies is to think about how you feel, and take the ones you need.

Formulas

People selling homeopathic and aromatherapy products often produce ready-made formulas that claim to contain everything needed for a particular condition or situation. Many writers on flower remedies have followed this cue and published flower remedy recipes for pregnancy and exams and other everyday situations. Whatever the merits of this approach in other therapies – and it is a contentious area – it rarely works as far as Bach Flower Remedies are concerned. The remedies are very personal, and treat individuals, not some pre-defined stereotype of what all people in a particular situation will feel.

Imagine a group of students preparing for an examination. Some feel sure they will fail. Others are scared of failing because of what their parents will say. Others feel so sure of success that they do not bother to revise properly. Others daydream and fail to take in what they are reading. Others rush through revision without taking time to learn anything. And so on and so on. It would be nonsense to pick four or five remedies and give the same mix to all of them.

There is only one recommended pre-mixed combination, and that is Rescue Remedy. This is an emergency mixture put together to help us through everyday crises. All the students could use Rescue Remedy to help them cope with their nerves as they go into the exam room. But they would need their own personal mixes to overcome the underlying imbalances that affected them in the weeks leading up to the exam. Rescue Remedy alone would be unlikely to contain the right combination of remedies.

Rescue Remedy and Rescue Cream

Rescue Remedy contains five single remedies.

- ■ Rock Rose – the remedy for terror and extreme fear.
- ■ Clematis – used to combat the faint, far-away, disconnected feelings that can come during an emergency.
- ■ Impatiens – for the agitation that accompanies adrenaline release.
- ■ Star of Bethlehem – to help deal with shock and loss.
- ■ Cherry Plum – to help the mind stay rational and in control.

Dr Bach created the first Rescue Remedy combination out of Rock Rose, Clematis and Impatiens, in about 1933. At that time Star of Bethlehem and Cherry Plum had not yet been discovered. In her biography of Dr Bach, Nora Weeks tells the story of one of the first times he used it, in the Norfolk fishing town of Cromer:

> On one occasion a man who had been strapped to the mast of a wrecked barge for five hours was brought ashore by the lifeboat. He was delirious, foaming at the mouth, helpless and almost frozen, his life despaired of.
>
> As he was being carried up the sands to a nearby house, Bach repeatedly moistened his lips with the Rescue Remedy, and before the man had been stripped of his clothing and wrapped in warm blankets he was sitting up and in his right mind, asking for a cigarette. He was taken to the hospital, but after a few days' rest he had completely recovered from his dreadful experience.

Rescue Remedy can be a life-saver, but you can also use it for any minor emergencies and crises, from receiving bad news to visiting the dentist. You can also buy it in a cream, introduced by Nora Weeks in the 1960s. Rescue Cream makes it easy to apply Rescue Remedy externally, and many people use it for rashes, grazes, bruises and so on. The cream includes Crab Apple as a cleanser – Crab Apple is the remedy for feeling unclean and unattractive, states that often accompany skin problems.

You might think that applying a cream to cuts and bruises violates the principle that the remedies only work on emotional imbalances, but in fact Dr Bach often applied remedies externally. If one of his patients had a broken leg and felt impatient to get back to work and worried over how his wife would cope, then Dr Bach might have given him Impatiens and Red Chestnut by mouth while applying the same remedies to the leg using a cold compress. He would have selected these remedies for the emotions (the impatience and anxiety) and not for the physical problem (the broken leg).

The same principle applies to all external use. If you fell downstairs you could take four drops of Rescue Remedy or add it to a cold compress or apply Rescue Cream to the affected area. Cold compresses and the cream in Rescue Cream *do* have a physical effect (the cold water helps any swelling go down and the cream is made in part from helpful natural healers such as honey) but the flower remedies in them treat the crisis of having fallen down the stairs, not the physical injuries.

Theoretically you could apply all the remedies in creams, or even make up a different cream for each of the 38. But for most purposes taking remedies by mouth is easier, and less messy.

Type remedies

We have seen how all the remedies act as mood remedies when they treat everyday emotions. Some also work at another level, describing characteristics, personalities and temperaments in addition to simple moods. Anyone can become over-enthusiastic about something, refuse to rest and burn the candle at both ends. The mood remedy for this is Vervain. But if you are someone who *tends to be* enthusiastic and *often* finds it hard to switch off you might be a Vervain type.

Other clear type remedies include:

- Mimulus – shy, timid people who feel anxious in social situations;
- Vine – strong, decisive leaders;
- Wild Rose – easy-going, relaxed people who drift through life;
- Impatiens – quick-thinking, active people who dislike delay;
- Oak – solid, dependable, methodical people who work steadily and without hurry;
- Water Violet – private, self-contained people, sometimes rather superior and proud;
- Heather – talkative people who are wrapped up in their lives;
- Rock Water – rigid-minded perfectionists who live by rules and targets.

This is not a complete list. There are other type remedies, and still others that only seem to indicate types. For example, Willow is for people who feel sorry for themselves and bitter about the way fate has treated them. The Willow state can look like a permanent characteristic until it is balanced, when it disappears and other personality traits appear in its place, or that at least is what most users of the remedies find. But we cannot say categorically that nobody will ever have a genuine Willow personality. This is why we can't draw up a definitive list of type remedies.

Knowing your type remedy tells you something about yourself and about the particular character weaknesses that you need to work on. It is part of learning about who you are. We all get impatient from time to time, but for a true Impatiens type impatience and hurry is a long-term problem. As an Impatiens type you can consciously try to develop your ability to stand still and savour life, and of course have the remedy near to hand when you are under stress.

How can you find out what type you are? One way is to imagine yourself in a stressful situation and analyse your emotional response. You might also think about the abilities and qualities you admire in other people, or ask yourself what you would like to change about yourself. What virtues do you lack? What vices do you have? Thinking about these questions and comparing your answers with remedy indications can go some way towards identifying your type remedy. But don't let it become an obsession. If you can't see your type clearly just take the remedies you need and don't worry whether they reflect characteristics or moods. Your type remedy will become apparent over time, and it may take time to get to it, especially if you have built up protective layers of emotional baggage.

EXERCISES

Identify your type remedy

A How do you define success? How do you go about achieving your definition of success?

B Think about someone you admire, either a contemporary or someone from history. Leaving aside his or her achievements, what is it about this person's character and approach to life that most appeals to you? Do you have some of that quality yourself?

C Under stress we sometimes say that we have 'lost it' or that we have not been able to cope. What do losing it and not coping mean to you?

D You have a free afternoon. You need to buy some milk from a supermarket half a mile away in a shopping centre, but apart from that you can do whatever you want. Going by what you have done in the past, how will the afternoon probably be spent? In an ideal world, how would you like it to be spent? What changes in your attitude or approach would make your afternoon more like the ideal?

E You have just started your free afternoon when a friend calls for a chat. How do you respond? How would you like to respond?

Selecting for long-term problems

Selecting for passing moods means passing into a metamood – standing aside from your emotions so as to see them better. Finding your type remedy means defining your basic personality and weaknesses. You use both skills when selecting remedies for long-term problems. Before looking at the process in detail, however, let's look at what we mean by long-term problems, and at how passing moods and personality imbalances create them.

If we live balanced and fulfilled lives our health tends to be good. We also cope better when things happen to knock us out of balance – and things do, all the time. We can even deal with very upsetting events like bereavement or losing our jobs. Sometimes, however, we do not recover from an out-of-balance state. Instead we adapt to it by distorting our personality to fit. Our emotional health suffers and we are more open to the development of other long-term negative states and physical illnesses. We may adopt different personae in order to cope with our situation, until we no longer recognize ourselves below our masks. Or we may choose not to be aware of a problem so as to avoid facing it, and this too causes strain and the development of yet more out-of-balance states.

The process by which negative emotions build up in layers is sometimes called the snowball effect – and it is the snowball effect that leads to long-term problems, both physical and emotional. Physical problems include any chronic condition or disease, or any extended period of general ill-health. Emotional problems include chronic anxiety, phobias, shyness, sadness, depression, long-term lack of confidence and so on. It should be clear how we can treat emotional problems using the remedies, so let us look more closely at physical problems, where it may not be so apparent how the remedies can help.

Most people who go to see Bach practitioners for the first time are suffering physical symptoms. Often they would like to walk out with a bottle that will remove the symptoms, and do not come prepared to talk about their emotional lives. Nevertheless, this is what practitioners ask them to do, because the practitioner's approach to illness, even physical illness, is to deal with its emotional causes. Uncovering the hidden mental wellspring of the physical condition takes pressure off the body so that it can go back to its natural state of health.

The process of revealing what was concealed is central to other therapies such as psychoanalysis and psychotherapy. Unlike some forms of those therapies, however, the remedies work very gently. They don't cause dramatic healing crises but instead slowly unpeel the emotional layers one at a time. Bach practitioners stay on the surface, asking at every point how the client feels *now*, until *now* is the heart of the problem. This process is a deliberate reversal of the snowball effect. It is called 'peeling the onion'.

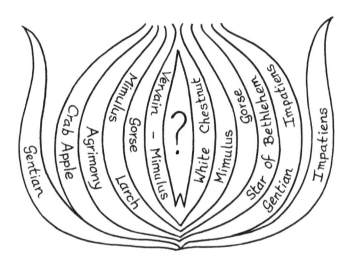

Figure 2.1 You only find out the centre of the problem once all the layers have been removed

What can you expect to find at the heart of your onion? Sometimes it will be your type remedy, which shows you the main personality quality that you need to work on. Other times it will be some traumatic event that was not adequately dealt with when it happened. Or it might be a trivial mood that grew out of all proportion. The only way to be sure is to start unpeeling, so, to sum up, here is how we can peel the onion of our own long-term problems:

1 Select the remedies we need for the way we feel now.
2 Take them regularly until they no longer apply.
3 Make a new selection.
4 Stop when you feel you don't need any remedies.

If you have mixed up a treatment bottle of remedies (see below) it will last about three weeks, so the end of a bottle is a good opportunity to look again at how you feel. Sometimes you might think that things have not changed, but find when you review the selection that you no longer need some of the remedies because those negative emotions have gone. If different emotions have been revealed – however out of balance they are – that is a sign of progress.

As we saw earlier, some people use dowsing, kinesiology and intuitive methods to select remedies. If they are successful they select for the heart of the problem right away, cutting to the centre of the onion instead of unpeeling it. The results can be dramatic, but there are real advantages to the slower approach. The most important is that it gives us the opportunity to learn about ourselves and our emotional history. The process enriches us and teaches us how we are likely to respond when things go wrong in future. Used properly, the remedies can give us an insight into who we really are.

Mixing and taking remedies

Shortly after Dr Bach had found the last of his 38 remedies a medical colleague suggested mixing them all together to make a single cure-all. Unfortunately this doesn't work. It seems that taking remedies you don't need stops those you do need from working efficiently. This is why you should try to restrict the number of remedies you take at any one time. Over the years, the Bach Centre has settled on a rule of thumb recommendation to take no more than six or seven remedies at the same time. This is not set in stone – sometimes eight remedies are needed, and we know that Dr Bach twice gave nine remedies in the same bottle. But for everyday purposes try to stick to the six to seven limit. (If you are mixing it in with other remedies, Rescue Remedy counts as one remedy.)

On most occasions you won't even need to take this many. As Nora Weeks used to say to people who asked about mixing remedies, if you feel only one is needed, be brave, take one. This is good advice. When one remedy is clear but you are not sure about a dozen or so others take the one you are sure of, and allow it to clear some of the fog away for you. Next time you will be better able to see which if any of the other 'possibles' are actually 'essentials'.

When you come to do the mixing you can use one of two basic methods. For passing moods take the remedies in a glass of water. First select the ones you want to take, then add two drops of each one to the glass. (The recommended dosage for Rescue Remedy is four drops instead of two.) Then sip from the glass at intervals until the mood has passed.

We are used to taking drugs that come wrapped in warnings about the risk of overdose and misuse. This makes us cautious about dosage, which is why so many questions come up on courses whenever a practitioner talks about taking the remedies. How big a glass of water should we use? How big is a sip? And how long is an interval – every few seconds or every few hours? The answer to all these questions is to stop worrying and do what seems right. The size of the glass is not relevant, nor is the size of the sip, because the amount of remedy added to the glass ensures that each sip will give you the equivalent of a minimum dose (see below). In an emergency you might take a sip every few seconds, and where the situation is less urgent you might only need to take a couple of sips during an evening.

You could use the glass of water method to treat long-term problems as well. If you want to do this be sure to sip from the glass at least four times a day, first thing in the morning, last thing at night, and two other times in between. You should also make up a fresh glass each morning in case the water has got dirty.

Most people using the remedies for long-term problems prefer to make up a treatment bottle. Treatment bottles use up less remedy, and are easier to carry around if you are out and about during the day. To make up a treatment bottle, buy an empty 30 ml or 1 oz dropper bottle from the shop where you bought your remedies. If you can't get this size any smaller size will do. Put two drops of each selected remedy into the bottle, and put in a double dose of Rescue Remedy if you are including that in the treatment. Top up the bottle with non-fizzy bottled mineral water and give it a little shake to mix the contents. Dosage from the treatment bottle is four drops, either direct on the tongue or in liquid, at least four times a day. Take the first dose first thing in the morning, the last one last thing at night, and the others at intervals in between. Four drops from a treatment bottle is the minimum dose. Taking less that this reduces the effectiveness of the remedies.

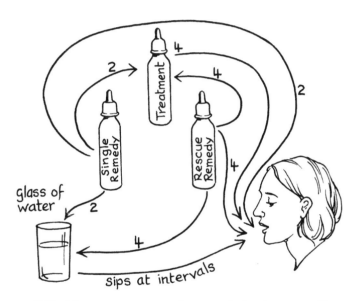

Figure 2.2 Always use two drops of single remedies and four drops of Rescue Remedy

A 30 ml treatment bottle will last up to three weeks. To help the water stay fresh you can keep the bottle in the refrigerator or any other cool place. Where this isn't possible, for example if you need to keep the treatment bottle in your car or pocket, add a preservative to the water. Most people use brandy – a 5 ml teaspoonful will do – but you can use any other strong spirit, or cider vinegar, or vegetable glycerine if you prefer.

In an emergency, when there is no water available, you can take undiluted remedies straight from the bottle. The dosage is two drops of the single remedies (four of Rescue Remedy) onto or under your tongue, and repeat as required. However, you should avoid this method when giving remedies to children and animals because of the brandy in the stock remedies.

People ask more questions about dosage than about any other subject. Some of the more common questions are covered in Chapter 12, but you won't go far wrong if you remember to take two drops out of single stock bottles, and four drops out of Rescue Remedy bottles and treatment bottles.

External applications

Applying remedies externally is less convenient than taking them by mouth, but it does work, and it may be the only option where someone is unconscious or not able to take any alcohol at all for religious or health reasons. Rub the drops into pulse points – wrist, temples, etc. You can also add two drops of single remedies (four of Rescue) to water to make cold or warm compresses, or put drops in the bath, something which many people find soothing.

Changing the mix

From time to time you will need to change the contents of the treatment bottle to reflect changes in your state of mind. If you are a few days into a treatment bottle when you decide to add an additional remedy, and assuming you still need the original selections, simply add two drops of the new remedy to the treatment bottle and go on taking it. Sometimes, however, you will want to add several new remedies and stop taking others. Or you may have finished the treatment bottle, and want to review the selection completely. In either case you need to make up a new bottle based on how you feel now. Leaving out any remedies that you no longer need will make room for new ones without your having to mix together more than six or seven.

You should sterilize treatment bottles before you re-use them. Bacteria will have got into the water, either from the air or from contact with your mouth or tongue, and you need to be sure they are clean. To sterilize a standard treatment bottle take it apart by unscrewing the top and pulling out the glass pipette and rubber teat. Then place the glass parts in a saucepan filled with enough cold water to cover the bottle. Bring this to the boil, then boil for 10 to 15 minutes. Remove the pan from the heat, drain and remove the bottle and pipette. Leave them to dry or, for a sparkling finish place them bottom up in a warm oven. It's usually enough to wash the plastic and rubber parts in hot soapy water and rinse them well. You can boil them if you think it necessary, but you will damage them if you do this too often.

You can also sterilize bottles using a steam or chemical sterilizer of the kind used for babies' bottles. Chemical sterilizers do leave a residue, however, and the contents taste of chemicals afterwards. If you want to use chemical or steam sterilizers follow the instructions issued by the manufacturer.

Integrating the remedies into healthcare

In a revised introduction to *The Twelve Healers and Other Remedies*, dictated just before his death, Dr Bach spoke of his discoveries as a complete system in its own right. 'This system of treatment is the most perfect which has been given to mankind within living memory,' he said. 'It has the power to cure disease; and, in its simplicity, it may be used in the household.'

The system is indeed perfect, not least because it can do no harm and is entirely positive in its effect. However, this does not mean it is the only way to approach health or that you should not take advantage of other therapies. There would be no point taking Mimulus to combat your fear of the dentist and then not having treatment to save your teeth. And peeling the onion and rediscovering your true self will not by itself repair physical damage that has already taken place, although it may help prevent further damage, and make you view what cannot be changed in a different way.

Far from denying the usefulness of other approaches to health, Dr Bach was a pioneer in some of them. He was ahead of his time in researching the effects of diet on long-term health, and one of the first to point out the similarities between vaccination and homeopathy. He recognized that orthodox and complementary approaches were all valid in their different ways, and would each have a part to play in a holistic healthcare plan. Use of the remedies should be part of an overall health strategy that may include a number of other approaches such as exercise, meditation, orthodox medicine, diet, and other complementary therapies.

The remedies fulfil this complementary role well. They are gentle and made entirely from non-toxic plants and there are no contraindications to the active ingredients. Even if you were highly allergic to nuts there would be no danger involved in taking a remedy like Walnut. The preparation methods used leave no trace of the actual plant in the stock bottles on the shelf. There is one contraindication, however, and this is to do with alcohol.

To make a remedy mother tincture the energized water is mixed 50:50 with 40 per cent proof brandy. The resulting mixture is further diluted at a ratio of two drops to 30 ml of 27 per cent proof brandy. This is the mix you buy in the shops. If you dilute the remedies into a treatment bottle and then take four drops from this four times a day you take in a minute amount of alcohol – just over half a drop for every remedy in the treatment bottle. This intake is spread over the life of the treatment bottle, typically two to three weeks, so for most purposes it can be disregarded, which is why the remedies are considered safe for pregnant women and small babies. Nevertheless some drugs carry a warning not to mix the contents with alcohol, so despite the low amounts of alcohol involved you may need to check with your qualified medical advisor before taking the remedies.

Two groups of people may have a particular problem: recovering alcoholics and people with a moral or religious objection to alcohol. Many recovering alcoholics feel reassured when they realize how little alcohol is involved. Even so, some decide not to take the four drops from the treatment bottle directly, but instead add them to a very hot drink such as tea or coffee so that the steam evaporates the tiny trace of alcohol. Others still do not feel happy about the possibility of taking any alcohol, and it is true that the psychological effect of feeling you are breaking a vow of total abstinence can far outweigh any physical consequences. If you are in this position you could consider applying the treatment bottle drops externally to the pulse points. Or you may feel that you would prefer not to take the remedies at all. If in doubt you should discuss the matter with your health advisor or alcohol counsellor.

Sometimes doctors prescribe a drug to recovering alcoholics that makes them sick if they drink alcohol. There are reports of people taking these drugs becoming ill without actually having a drink. Even applying an alcohol-based after-shave could cause a problem. If you have been prescribed a drug to help you stay off alcohol you should check with the person who prescribed the drug before you use the remedies, even externally. Drug companies make a number of such preparations. The most common in the UK is sold under the name Antabuse.

People with a moral or religious objection to alcohol may find a solution in adding remedies to boiling drinks or using them externally. Some religions give special dispensation for the medical use of alcohol. Consult your spiritual advisor if you are not sure where you stand.

EXERCISES

Taking remedies

For the purpose of this exercise you will need one or two remedies – take a look at the glossary and pick out a couple that strike a chord with you – plus a bottle of Rescue Remedy and a 30 ml (or smaller) dropper bottle.

A Read up on the indications for Rescue Remedy. Carry Rescue Remedy about with you for a day. When you feel that things are getting on top of you take some Rescue and think about what it does for you.

B Look up the indications for the single remedy or remedies that you have chosen. Keep your chosen remedies in your pocket for a week, and use them when you feel you need to. As before, notice what effect they have on you.

C Try mixing up a dummy treatment bottle using the remedies you have. (Remember to put in four drops of Rescue Remedy, but two drops each of all the others.)

Recap

■ You need to be able to identify your emotions if you want to use the remedies successfully.

■ All 38 remedies are mood remedies, used to address everyday emotional imbalances.

■ Rescue Remedy, the one pre-mixed combination available, helps during emergency situations.

■ Rescue Cream is an external application of Rescue Remedy plus Crab Apple.

■ Some remedies are type or personality remedies, because as well as moods they also describe characteristics and temperaments.

■ You should aim to use no more than six or seven remedies at a time.

■ The two main methods of taking the remedies are in a glass of water and via a treatment bottle.

■ Negative emotions tend to build up in layers. Successive mixes of remedies strip off these layers one by one in a process known as 'peeling the onion'.

■ You should boil treatment bottles before re-use to ensure they are clean.

■ The remedies are complementary medicines, and can be used safely alongside any other therapy.

■ Remedies contain alcohol, so if you are especially sensitive to this you may need to take further advice before using them.

3 | LEARNING THE REMEDIES

Aims of this chapter

This chapter explains why you should learn all 38 remedies by heart, and suggests ways you can learn to 'think Bach'.

■ The advantages of learning the remedies.
■ Observing yourself and others.
■ Learning from history and fiction.

Why bother learning the remedies?

You wouldn't learn all the colours on a paint chart. Instead you would look through a brochure when you needed some paint, and choose some suitable colours. The equivalent with the remedies would be to read the indications in a book every time you felt you needed a remedy, until you found the ones that seemed to fit. Some beginners don't even go this far, and rely entirely on the one-word indications found in leaflets picked up at health food shops. Neither approach is satisfactory. On a superficial level many of the remedies seem similar, and without in-depth knowledge you will find it difficult to decide between them. Moreover, you will soon tire of reading 38 paragraphs every time you want a remedy. Either you will stop using them, or you will confine yourself to the three or four that you remember and miss out remedies that you need.

There is no substitute for learning the remedies. You will be able to spend more time thinking about your feelings rather than about the mechanics of a half-remembered system. And when you know the remedies you will have learned a flexible language with which to think about who you are and how you feel, so that studying the system becomes a step towards greater self-awareness.

Starting in the next chapter you will find descriptions of all the remedies along with exercises to help you learn them. But before this, let's look at the opportunities in our everyday lives to practise remedy selection. Many of them demand little or no effort and can be incorporated into our normal everyday activities.

Observation

Most of us come into contact with hundreds of people every day. Use this to your advantage, and practise your remedy knowledge on the people you meet. This need not be obtrusive and you don't need to act differently, just look at what is going on around you and think about what remedies might apply.

For example, you might spend your journey to work looking for people in an Impatiens state – they are easy to spot in the rush hour. You will soon have a set of clear images showing what an Impatiens state looks like. Use your family and friends as well. Look down the list of remedies and pick out those that match Uncle George or your sister or your sister's boyfriend. And be aware of your own moods. Being conscious of a remedy state – and resolving it by taking that remedy – teaches its own lesson. Some people like to keep a diary of their observations and remedy states. A remedy journal could also record which remedies you took and when, and any effects you noticed. And don't forget to include remarks made by your friends and family, as they often notice changes in our states of mind before we do.

EXERCISES
Observation
  A Go back to the previous chapter and have another go at the exercises 'to identify your type remedy'. Then look through the glossary at the end of the book and try to find the remedies that best fit your answers.
  B Pick a day when you will be out and about – either shopping, or going to work or school – and on that

day try to spot other people who seem to need the remedies you identified in the previous question. What is it about them that tells you they need those remedies?

C Think about the two people you know best in the world, and the way they handle problems. Use the glossary to suggest remedies they might need.

History and fiction as learning aids

People can be complex and difficult to pin down. Rather than observe real people, then, you may find it easier at first to work with caricatures of the kind found in many television programmes. Soap operas and situation comedies are good for this, since both rely on broadly drawn and distinctive characters. You don't need to make a special study of television drama, just watch what you would normally watch, but with the remedies in mind. Spotting Vine and Centaury characters will soon become second nature.

Written fiction works just as well. Most authors – certainly in more traditional forms – provide complete character descriptions that will help you identify remedies. If your taste runs to non-fiction you will find biographies and history books useful, as they too rely to some extent on simplification and character study. You can also study magazine interviews with famous people, or simply think about a famous person and try to imagine which remedies would apply. Finally, don't forget fairy stories, which often turn on archetypes that are wonderfully close to classic remedy descriptions. Once you have hit on a good incarnation of a remedy you will find it much easier to remember that remedy in future. If you know that the biblical character Samson is an Oak type, you know at once what that remedy is for, almost without having to read the indications.

EXERCISES

Using stories

A Record a favourite TV programme. Watch it one scene at a time, and with the aid of the glossary at the end of the book try to match remedies to the different personality types and passing moods that are portrayed.

B Read this extract from Charles Dickens' *Sketches by Boz*, and use the glossary to suggest some remedies that might have a positive effect on the four Miss Willises:

> The house was the perfection of neatness – so were the four Miss Willises. Everything was formal, stiff, and cold – so were the four Miss Willises. Not a single chair of the whole set was ever seen out of its place – not a single Miss Willis of the whole four was ever seen out of hers. There they always sat, in the same places, doing precisely the same things at the same hour. The eldest Miss Willis used to knit, the second to draw, the two others to play duets on the piano. They seemed to have no separate existence, but to have made up their minds just to winter through life together. . . . Whatever the eldest did, the others did, and whatever anybody else did, they all disapproved of; and thus they vegetated – living in Polar harmony among themselves, and, as they sometimes went out, or saw company 'in a quiet-way' at home, occasionally icing the neighbours.

C Using the glossary as a guide, find remedies for these famous people and fictional characters: 1) Hamlet; 2) Joan of Arc; 3) Adolf Hitler; 4) Mahatma Gandhi; 5) John Lennon; 6) Don Quixote; 7) Charlie Chaplin; 8) Winston Churchill; 9) Cinderella; 10) Snow White's wicked stepmother.

Thinking Bach

Think again about Dr Bach's remark, that using the remedies should be as simple and natural as eating lettuce. The only way to achieve this is if we know almost by instinct when to use each of the remedies. Is this possible?

I believe it is, because the remedy indications are categories, and we think in categories all the time. Psychoanalysts classify parts of people's personalities in terms of id, ego and superego; psychologists talk of extroverts and introverts; politicians talk about right, left and centre; and music fans divide their subject into rock, pop, hip-hop, rhythm 'n' blues, blues, jazz, jazz-funk, funk, disco, techno, choral, orchestral, chamber music and skiffle. All of these terms have passed into everyday language. We use them to think about and describe the world, even if we have little understanding of the theory behind them – we know jazz when we hear it even if few of us could define it without the aid of a book. When the remedies are as normal to our way of thinking as categories of music, then we really know the system, and can start to think Bach – in other words, think *with* the remedies, instead of just thinking *about* them.

Recap

■ Learning the remedies helps you focus on your emotions, and leads to greater self-awareness.

■ Everyday activities like social events, watching television and reading books can all provide opportunities for learning to 'think Bach'.

Answers to exercises

Using stories

B Several remedies could apply. Your selection might include Beech, Rock Water and Crab Apple.

C Again, you might have chosen different answers. My suggestions are: 1) Scleranthus; 2) Rock Water; 3) Vine, Cherry Plum, Holly; 4) Rock Water; 5) Vervain; 6) Clematis; 7) Agrimony; 8) Oak; 9) Centaury; 10) Holly, Vine.

4 | THE REMEDIES: FEAR AND WORRY

Aims of this chapter

In the final edition of Dr Bach's book on the remedies, *The Twelve Healers and Other Remedies*, he grouped them under seven headings. The first category was 'for those who have fear'. He placed five remedies in this group.

- Red Chestnut – in Dr Bach's words, 'for those who find it difficult not to be anxious for other people'.
- Mimulus – 'the fears of everyday life'.
- Rock Rose – 'in accident or sudden illness, or when the patient is very frightened or terrified'.
- Aspen – 'vague, unknown fears, for which there can be given no explanation'.
- Cherry Plum – 'fear of the mind being over-strained'.

In this chapter we will consider all these, plus some remedies (from other groups) that relate to fear, anxiety and worry. At what point does a worrying thought become an anxious one? We will find the answer in the boundary between White Chestnut and Mimulus.

- White Chestnut – classed under the heading 'Not Sufficient Interest in Present Circumstances', this is for people beset by worrying thoughts.
- Larch – Dr Bach placed this remedy for people who fear failure in the 'Despondency or Despair' category.
- Agrimony – listed under 'Over-sensitive to Influences and Ideas', this is for people who hide their worries behind good humour.

This chapter and the next five introduce the 38 remedies. They use stories – many based on real-life situations – to illustrate the kind of emotions that the remedies help to rebalance. Some of the examples mention physical symptoms, and re-balancing emotions can indirectly help physical problems. Nevertheless, the remedies are not cures for specific physical conditions, and there is no relationship between any named remedy and any named medical condition.

Red Chestnut

Gwynneth and her husband tried for a baby for several years, and had several IVF treatments. At last they had a success, and they told their family she was expecting. Everyone was delighted. Gwynneth's mother Evelyn, who only lived half a mile away, offered to help get the house ready and generally make herself useful.

At first Gwynneth was grateful for her mother's help, but after a time she began to dread her daily visits. Evelyn would not allow her to do anything. She cleaned the house, shopped, cooked dinner and even started decorating the nursery. She pushed Gwynneth into a chair in front of the television every morning, and stopped any attempt at more strenuous activity with a smile and the words 'Don't worry, I'll do that.'

After swallowing her annoyance for a time, Gwynneth eventually told her mother how unhappy she was with the way things were going. For the first time Evelyn told her daughter about suffering a late miscarriage a year after her marriage. She was terrified that the same thing would happen to Gwynneth, and this is why she wrapped her daughter in cotton wool and would not allow her to take risks.

Remedy description

Red Chestnut is for people who worry about the welfare of others, usually relations or friends. The fear can be out of all proportion to the real risk and lead to over-protective behaviour that harms the confidence and independence of the people being worried over.

We can see Red Chestnut in the way parents drive their children to school instead of letting them walk as they used to do. Thanks to a more active and available media, we see more reports of violent crime and offences against children than our parents did. We worry more about our children, and as a result they get less exercise and miss out on the chance to learn independence.

The Red Chestnut type has an in-built tendency to worry over other people more than usual, but all of us can fall into a Red Chestnut state. The remedy helps to put our fears into perspective. Instead of spreading our concern to the people around us and undermining their confidence we can reassure them and help them grow. We radiate confidence and positive thinking, and anxiety is a thing of the past.

The Red Chestnut remedy is made using the boiling method and the pink-red flowers of *Aesculus carnea.*

Case discussion

At first Evelyn's behaviour doesn't look like Red Chestnut at all, and a Bach practitioner might consider Chicory, the remedy for people who like looking after their loved ones and being the centre of family life. Red Chestnut comes through when we discover the reason for her behaviour, namely her fear that something will happen to her daughter and her unborn grandchild. Chicory people overprotect to demonstrate how important and needed they are; Red Chestnut people genuinely do not think of themselves, and their care is all for others.

Evelyn might need other remedies as well. Agrimony might have helped her talk sooner about her feelings rather than hiding them. Star of Bethlehem, the remedy for shock and loss, might also help. The miscarriage was a long time ago but Evelyn's behaviour suggests that it has not been adequately dealt with. As for Gwynneth, Centaury might have helped her stand up sooner for what she wanted.

Mimulus

Nathan worked as a technical author for a company that trained people to use computer software. He produced all the course materials that the trainers used. He was a quiet person, and liked the fact that his job did not require him to meet clients face to face.

There was a flu virus going around, and within the space of half an hour late one Tuesday afternoon three trainers phoned in to say that they would not be able to teach their scheduled courses the next day. One of the Sales team volunteered to teach the beginners' spreadsheet course; and the company's systems administrator took over the Local Area Network course. That left one course with no tutor, and the only person in the company who knew how to use the latest web site developer kit was Nathan, who had written the training course. He felt he had no option but to say yes, because he couldn't bear to admit that he was scared of standing up in front of a room full of strangers. He went home that night with his stomach in knots, and spent a sleepless night.

The next morning Nathan got to work an hour earlier than usual and tried to plan how the course would go. But five minutes before it was due to start he escaped to the toilet and threw up. Locked in the cubicle, he thought seriously about leaving the building and the job so as to avoid having to step into that classroom.

Remedy description

Mimulus is the remedy for any fear or anxiety that has a definite, nameable cause. Fear of the dark, of rats, of public speaking, of redundancy, and of being mugged would all be Mimulus fears.

The remedy encourages the natural strength and quiet courage that lie within all of us. It helps us face up to our anxieties and work through them. It centres us so that we can face the world and the rest of humanity without fear, knowing that nothing can hurt us if we have faith in ourselves. As a type remedy it helps shy, quiet people who like to avoid being noticed in public. Typically a true Mimulus type does not share her fears with others but keeps them to herself, attempting to deal with them on her own.

The Mimulus remedy is made using the sun method and the bright yellow flowers of *Mimulus guttatus*.

Case discussion

Rescue Remedy would help keep Nathan calm, but it would not address the underlying problem, which is his shyness and fear of speaking in public. The remedy for this would be Mimulus. In addition he might consider Centaury to help him say 'no' when he wanted to, and White Chestnut would have helped if he spent his sleepless night going over and over what he had to do in the morning.

Rock Rose

Georgina left the children alone for only a moment while she went to get ice creams. During the few minutes that she was at the other side of the park three-year-old Darren managed to get to the top of the big slide. His three sisters were busy playing on the swings and didn't notice. Coming back with the ice creams, Georgina saw a middle-aged lady bending down over something on the floor. Then she saw the three girls running over towards the same shape, and only then did she realize that it was Darren.

He was pale and not moving. That was all she saw before the fear swept over her, freezing her mind on the icy impossibility of explaining to his mother what had happened. He was dead, he was dead. Life was over and there was no way round it. Meanwhile the middle-aged lady sat Darren up and checked him over. She quieted him and the crying girls by taking the ice creams from Georgina's hands and giving them out. Then she gave Georgina something from a small brown bottle.

Remedy description

Rock Rose is the remedy for absolute terror. The Rock Rose fear is normally of something specific, but it is far stronger than the Mimulus fear and leaves its victim unable to think coherently. Even when the external cause appears trivial the inner state is dramatic, overwhelming us and leading to panic, or to a frozen terror in which we are unable to act at all.

The Rock Rose remedy comes from the papery, pale yellow flowers of *Helianthemum nummularium*. These are prepared using the sun method. It helps unlock even the greatest fear so that we are better able to deal with it.

Case discussion

The good Samaritan probably gave the emergency combination Rescue Remedy to Georgina. Of its five ingredients the main ones she needed were Rock Rose and Star of Bethlehem, the remedies for terror and shock respectively. People often combine these two in emergency situations, but there may well be terror without shock, as for example when a long terminal illness reaches its last stages. Rock Rose helps the bystanders and the person going through the experience – terror is an infectious emotion, and spreads quickly. In this case Georgina would probably have got over her terror anyway, seeing that Darren was not seriously hurt, but thanks to Rock Rose recovery came more quickly.

Aspen

Jenny was an agency nurse hired to live-in three days a week with an old couple, both of whom were disabled. The couple were welcoming enough, although they had been used in the past to having paid servants and did not always see that Jenny wasn't one of them. They gave her an attic room to sleep in.

The room was small and dark, with one tiny window that looked out over fields and hills. During the day Jenny admired the view and thought it beautiful, but the room itself seemed gloomy and oppressive. At night the blank window seemed to stare at her, and she worked herself up to the point that she hated going to bed at night. She slept with the light on and the covers pulled over her head, the hair bristling on the back of her neck. Not usually superstitious, she felt there was some undefined presence in the room. Perhaps it was haunted.

The fear was growing worse. She thought about quitting. But the agency would ask why she wanted to leave, and she couldn't give any real reason for her fears beyond a general feeling that something wasn't right.

Remedy description

Aspen treats vague, unnamed fears, where there seems nothing to be afraid of and no definite cause for anxiety. The Aspen fear ranges from a mild sense of unease all the way up to a complete terror, but in all cases the cause is undefined.

Some states include a mix of Aspen and Mimulus. Fear of the dark is one. It is a Mimulus fear because it is fear of something definite, but where there are elements of the supernatural – something nameless in the dark – then Aspen applies as well.

Some authors class Aspen as a type remedy, indicated for especially sensitive and spiritual people who easily feel spooked. But most practitioners agree that people who look like Aspen types at first tend to display different characteristics once the Aspen state has been resolved.

The aspen tree *Populus tremula* is used to make this remedy. The tree is known for its delicate leaves, each one attached by a long slender stalk that sets the leaves quivering in the slightest wind. The catkins used to make the remedy are prepared using the boiling method.

Case discussion

The fact that Jenny cannot give a clear reason for her fears suggests Aspen as the correct remedy to give, rather than any of the possible alternatives.

EXERCISES

Red Chestnut, Mimulus, Rock Rose and Aspen

Look at these situations and in each case choose either Red Chestnut, Mimulus, Rock Rose or Aspen for the main character.

A A four-year-old has started his first day at school and is scared when his mother tries to leave.

B His mother spends all day worrying over how he is getting on.

C A 12-year-old watches a horror film at a friend's house, then runs all the way home in the dark.

D Trying to conquer his fear of flying, a middle-aged man manages to get on the plane. Panic overtakes him just before take-off, and he runs down the aisle and off the plane, not caring that everyone is looking at him.

Cherry Plum

All through his teenage years Christopher quarrelled with his father. The subject was usually politics: Christopher took a left-wing view while his father's sympathies were more to the right. His father couldn't resist making comments when the early evening news came on, and Christopher always rose to the bait. Dinner usually turned into a shouting match, which would end only when Christopher stormed out of the house, slamming the door to relieve his feelings.

That was 20 years ago. Now Christopher is married with two children. His father who was widowed six years ago has come to stay following a stroke. Christopher thought he would be able to cope with his father now – he isn't a teenager any more – but the old patterns are re-establishing themselves. He loses his temper even worse than before, and a few times has found himself pounding the table with his fists, frightening his two boys, because it is the only way he can stop himself from striking his father. The strength of his own emotions terrifies him and he worries that he will lose control and attack the old man.

Remedy description

Cherry Plum helps people who fear they will lose their self-control and do some injury either to themselves or to someone else. A good example of a Cherry Plum state is the child in a tantrum, who screams blue murder at his mother but underneath is terrified of how he feels, and just wants to be picked up and soothed back to reason. Cherry Plum helps restore reason to people who are behaving irrationally and threatening to commit acts of violence.

The Cherry Plum remedy is made from the fresh white blossom that appears on the *Prunus cerasifera* tree early in the spring. Preparation is by the boiling method.

Case discussion

Christopher feels frightened of something specific, which might suggest Mimulus or Rock Rose as possible remedies. But when we look at the cause of the fear, which is his lack of control, we can see that Cherry Plum fits better. It will help Christopher tame his impulsive, irrational temper, so that he can start thinking about what might be causing it. This may lead him to take other remedies, such as Beech to give him more tolerance or Walnut to help him resist the slide back into old behaviour patterns. Vervain would probably have applied in the past, given the fact that family disagreements were often over beliefs and values, so this too would be a remedy worth exploring.

Larch

Ben went to university after achieving excellent grades at his school exams. He studied computer science, and early on his teachers predicted that he would finish with a first class or upper second degree. But he didn't do very much work at university, and concentrated on his social life. In the end he graduated with a third class degree, and only got that after re-submitting his final assessment.

From then on he avoided computers. He worked behind a bar for a time. Then he spent a year on a building site, carrying bricks for a friend, and finished up helping another friend plant, prune and chop down trees. When he met up with people who had known him at university they were surprised that he wasn't working with computers – they were well aware that for the first year of the course he had been top of every class. But Ben just shrugged. He knew he would make a mess of anything that required academic ability, so he was going to leave that to them.

Remedy description

Larch is the remedy for lack of confidence. People in this state do not take up challenges because they are convinced that they are going to fail. Sometimes they draw comfort from this certainty, and use it as a way of retreating from life and staying in their comfort zone. Sometimes they are desperate to try for success, but turn aside because they have so little confidence in their abilities. Another indication often given for Larch is 'fear of failure'. What this means is that the Larch person may be frightened of not doing something well and choose to avoid the possibility by not trying in the first place.

The mention of a nameable fear highlights the subtle relationship between Larch and Mimulus, two remedies often given together. Imagine you are worrying over having to give a speech – would the correct remedy be Mimulus for a known anxiety, or Larch to give the confidence needed to take the platform? Or should you take both? A simple test involves answering two questions: 'Are you frightened of what may happen to you if you do this?' and 'Do you think you are capable of doing it well?' If the answer to the first question is yes, take Mimulus. If the answer to the second is no, take Larch.

The tree used to make the Larch remedy, *Larix decidua*, is unusual in that it is the only conifer to shed its leaves in winter. The catkins are prepared using the boiling method.

Case discussion

Ben hides behind his supposed lack of ability in order to avoid having to test himself and so risk further failure. He could do well in the computer industry, but finds it more comfortable to avoid the challenge. Larch is his main remedy and there might be an argument for his taking Wild Rose, Gentian or Gorse, depending on the exact nature of the lethargy and discouragement that seem to accompany the main Larch state.

EXERCISES

Mimulus, Rock Rose, Larch and Cherry Plum

Decide which out of Mimulus, Rock Rose, Larch and Cherry Plum might apply to these situations.

A Peter would like to go on a working holiday rebuilding dry stone walls in a conservation area. What puts him off is the accommodation – shared dormitories – and the communal life. He feels uncomfortable having to live with strangers.

B His friend is reluctant for a different reason. She is no good with her hands, and any wall she tries to build is bound to fall over in the first strong wind.

C A teacher has a phobia of birds. During the mid-morning break, while she is catching up on some marking, a pigeon gets in through one of the high windows and begins to fly around the room. She rushes to the door in such a panic that she cannot get it open properly, and scratches herself badly on the latch when she finally wrenches it open.

White Chestnut

Mike trained as a settler – someone who settles bets on horse races – and passed the final test with a 100 per cent score. During the training course and the exam the students were not allowed to use calculators. Mike was so proud of his ability to calculate bets in his head that when he got a job in a betting shop he didn't use a calculator like everyone else, but carried on using mental arithmetic.

Saturday was the busiest day of the week, with a shop full of people and racing all day and well into the evening. Every Saturday night Mike would suffer from insomnia as he calculated bets in his head over and over again: £4 win at 7/2; a £20 double at 6/4 and 8/11; a Lucky 15 at 10/1, 6/4, 11/8 and 5/2 . . .

Remedy description

White Chestnut is for unwanted, persistent, worrying thoughts. They can be worries in the full meaning of the word, such as when we continually think about a fearful situation or the welfare of someone else, and in these cases there is likely to be an element of Mimulus or Red Chestnut as well. But White Chestnut worries are not necessarily fearful. They can just as well be mental arguments, or come when we replay real or imagined scenes over and over in our heads.

The key to White Chestnut is that the thoughts are repetitive and circular, and that they stop us from concentrating on the here and now. When they come at night they may cause insomnia, while during the day we might find it difficult to concentrate on what we should be doing.

The White Chestnut remedy is made from the flowers of the chestnut tree *Aesculus hippocastanum*. These are prepared using the sun method.

Case discussion

Mike's sleeplessness suggests we consider White Chestnut, but many other remedy states could lead to sleepless nights. In this case his enthusiasm for his work raises the possibility of Vervain, another state that can lead to hyper-activity of the mind. White Chestnut is preferred because of the circular nature of his mental activity and its essential meaninglessness.

Agrimony

Tom was single and in his mid forties. He worked as a salesman in the food industry. His week was taken up with endless meetings, and he often took clients out to lunch and dinner in order to smooth the way to a good relationship. He had been feeling a little unwell for some time, and suffered from chronic diarrhoea, but pushed health worries to one side and carried on with life. Then one day he found blood in his stool and finally went to see the doctor.

The diagnosis when it came hit him like a lead weight: cancer of the bowel, and he should go into hospital for exploratory surgery. But Tom put it off. He had lots of important clients to see. He buried himself in work, attending out of town conferences and arranging extra meetings. His entertaining expenses went through the roof.

Some clients had heard about his diagnosis – the leak had come from a colleague at the office – but if any of them asked how his treatment was going he would make a joke about only going to the hospital to see the nurses. They were phoning him every day they were so keen to see him again. This was true enough. He had already missed two appointments.

Remedy description

Agrimony is both a type and mood remedy. Classic Agrimony types seem happy and outgoing. No matter what is happening in their lives they will put a brave face on it, and either make a joke or pass on to lighter topics. They are known as peacemakers because they do not like unpleasantness and try to smooth over conflict, both in their own lives and in the lives of those around them.

Many remedy types will tend not to open up or share troubles – Water Violet, Mimulus and Impatiens people will all, for different reasons, tend to keep things to themselves. What sets Agrimony people apart is the smiling face they wear when things go wrong, and the fact that they don't hide themselves away. On the contrary, they seek out social activity as a way of not being alone with their thoughts. They may also turn to drink and other drugs in an effort to blot out and bury their woes.

Anyone can get into an Agrimony state in the right circumstances. Perhaps we feel obliged to appear brave and unaffected so as not to upset someone else, perhaps it is a role forced on us because of our job or the part we are playing in a crisis. Whatever the reason, Agrimony can help us to get to grips with our inner torment and pain, and deal with them more effectively.

Agrimony is made using the sun method from the yellow flowering spikes of *Agrimonia eupatoria*.

Case discussion

Tom was in an Agrimony state, and quite probably was an Agrimony type. The reaction to the diagnosis of cancer was typical, and contained many of the archetypal Agrimony elements, such as making a joke of things, refusing to face up to them, and trying not to spend too much time alone. The practitioner in this case considered suggesting Hornbeam – the remedy among other things for procrastination – because Tom was putting off going into hospital, but decided against it because Tom wasn't so much delaying treatment as avoiding it, and Agrimony already covered that.

She did choose two other remedies for Tom. The first was Star of Bethlehem, for the undigested shock of the diagnosis, and the other was Rock Rose, since when he did talk about the cancer he seemed unable to think clearly and was plainly terrified.

EXERCISES
Agrimony and White Chestnut

Read these descriptions of people in difficult circumstances and decide whether Agrimony or White Chestnut would be the better choice. Would any of the other remedies in this chapter also help?

A After hearing the news about his redundancy Jimmy seems distracted and doesn't do much work in the afternoon.

B Ten minutes later his colleague Ray emerges from his interview and invites everyone to the pub for a farewell drink – they can come and help him spend the redundancy money.

C Another colleague, Muriel, has not had her interview yet. Trying to work out whether the axe will fall, she sits alone going over all the mistakes she might have made since she joined the company. She also rehearses what her husband will say when he finds out that she is out of work.

Other fear and worry remedies

If you seem preoccupied because you can't stop thinking about a project at work, and the thoughts are constructive and due to your over-enthusiasm, then Vervain would apply. If you worried about the welfare of someone you loved, but did this for self-interested reasons – in other words you wanted to feel needed – then Chicory would apply. These examples show how you might use the words 'fear' and 'worry' and actually mean something rather different.

■ 'I'm afraid that I will never get better' might mean you have given up hope, which would indicate Gorse.

■ 'I'm worried that I will not be able to cope with all the extra work' could be an indication for Elm.

■ 'I'm worried that I will make the wrong decision – what do you think I should do?' might lead you to consider Cerato.

■ 'I get anxious if I am kept waiting' could be a way of describing impatience and agitation, and this would suggest Impatiens.

■ 'I worry over what other people will think' could be an indication for Centaury or Walnut.

We will consider these remedies in later chapters. For the present, keep in mind that the fear and worry remedies introduced in this chapter aren't the only ones to consider when you use those words to describe how you feel. Words are slippery. Different people use different words to describe the same feeling, or cover different feelings under the same word. When selecting remedies the feeling beneath the words is the final guide.

EXERCISES

Fear and worry

After a lot of pressure from his two teenage sons, a father has agreed to take them on a skiing holiday. Suggest more details of his situation, actions or feelings, assuming that he needs these remedies.

A Red Chestnut.

B Mimulus.

C Rock Rose.

D Aspen.

E Cherry Plum.

F Larch.

G White Chestnut.

H Agrimony.

Recap

■ Dr Bach isolated five specific remedies for fear: Mimulus, Aspen, Red Chestnut, Rock Rose and Cherry Plum.

■ Other remedies often used for different types of fear and worry are Larch, White Chestnut and Agrimony.

- Red Chestnut helps people who become worried and anxious about the welfare of people they love.
- Mimulus is the remedy for any fear with a clear and identifiable cause.
- Rock Rose treats extreme terror, such as might be found at the scene of an accident or where violence has been committed.
- Aspen helps counteract vague feelings of foreboding, and any fear where there is no clear cause.
- Cherry Plum helps us stay on top of our emotions when we fear we will lose control.
- Larch helps people who fear and expect failure.
- White Chestnut calms repetitive, worrying thoughts.
- Agrimony is for people who worry in secret but hide from their fears by making a joke of things.

Answers to exercises

Red Chestnut, Mimulus, Rock Rose and Aspen

A Mimulus is most likely.

B Red Chestnut.

C If he is scared of something specific in the film, Mimulus. If his is a supernatural, nameless terror, Aspen.

D Rock Rose.

Mimulus, Rock Rose, Larch and Cherry Plum

A Mimulus.

B Larch.

C Rock Rose and Cherry Plum.

Agrimony and White Chestnut

A White Chestnut, on the assumption that he is going over what has happened in his mind and is unable to concentrate.

B Agrimony.

C White Chestnut. Mimulus might help as well.

Fear and worry

Here are my suggestions. Yours may be different, but the emotions you describe should be similar.

A He is worried that they will be injured.

B He has never skied before, and is anxious about injuring himself.

C He is 100 yards away when he sees one of them hit by another skier and thrown onto some rocks.

D The holiday is going well, but he feels uneasy.

E He goes berserk and lashes out when he finds drugs in the elder boy's ski suit.

F He has never skied before, and sits around the ski centre all day rather than try lessons.

G He is unable to stop going over the argument he had with his wife just before they left.

H He fears his wife is seeing a lover while they are away, but plays the clown to keep the boys amused.

5 | THE REMEDIES: DEPRESSION AND HOPE

Aims of this chapter

The word 'depression' applies to a whole range of emotions, from the mild discouragement we feel at missing a train to major depression, a serious mental illness with a variety of symptoms including guilt, delusions, fatigue, malnutrition and exaggerated fears. A major depression would call for a number of different remedies and would also require qualified medical help. We concentrate in this chapter on minor depression, a more common state that includes deep feelings of sadness and anguish, such as we might feel after a bereavement, as well as milder forms of pessimism. We will look in detail at six remedies that are commonly associated with these states.

- Gentian – Dr Bach placed this in the 'Uncertainty' category, and said it was for people who become discouraged when things go wrong.
- Gorse – another from the same category, this helps people who believe that nothing can be done for them.
- Sweet Chestnut – listed by Dr Bach in the group of remedies that were for 'Despondency or Despair', this is for great and unbearable anguish.
- Oak – another 'Despondency or Despair' remedy, this is for strong, steady people who struggle on through every adversity.
- Mustard – classed under 'Not Sufficient Interest in Present Circumstances', this is for people who occasionally feel full of gloom when there seems every reason to be happy.

■ Willow – a 'Despondency or Despair' remedy, for those who feel resentment when things go wrong, and complain about the good fortune of others.

Gentian

Hannah worked as a translator in the London branch of a large German bank, up until her first child was born. Years later, when her third child started full-time education, she felt the time had come to return to work. She would not be able to go back full-time because she still had child care responsibilities. So she decided to set up as a freelance translator.

She called a few old friends in the business, but it was the first time she had tried to contact them in 12 years. Not only had individuals moved, but whole departments and companies had disappeared. Eventually she tracked down a former colleague and they arranged to meet for lunch.

She arrived at the bistro full of hope but by the end of the meal felt rather downcast. Everything in banking and translation had changed beyond recognition. Instead of letters and couriers, work was sent and received over the internet. Clients now expected documents to arrive formatted and laid out ready for the printer. Hannah had never even used a computer. Even banking had changed. The computer was king here as well, and business was done in euros.

By the time she got home from her lunch date Hannah felt like giving up.

Remedy description

Gentian gives encouragement to people who have suffered a setback, and helps them rise above and overcome their circumstances. It helps us see that with a little more faith we can avoid despondency and find a way forward.

The Gentian state is a mild, low feeling, and usually thought of as a passing mood rather than a personality trait. Indeed, there is some disagreement as to whether Gentian can ever be a type remedy. There are those who say it can point to people who tend to get discouraged easily, while others do not consider being discouraged a strong personality characteristic in its own right and look for the person's true personality to come through once the Gentian state has been addressed.

The Gentian remedy is made using the sun method and the blue-violet flowers of the autumn gentian, *Gentiana amarella*.

Case discussion

Hannah has suffered a setback and as a result feels downhearted and slightly depressed. This emotion will not damage her long-term outlook on life and will probably go by itself in time. But while it lasts it feels real enough, and it stops her getting on with her life.

In a positive state of mind Hannah would do something about her situation. The exact solution could be anything from trying a different career to asking one of her sons to teach her word processing – but whatever solution she decides to adopt she will not find it until she starts looking. Gentian will give her the encouragement she needs to get started. It is the only remedy she needs at the moment. It could be that she will have trouble adjusting to the many changes in her profession, and if she does then Walnut will help her. But until she begins adapting we cannot know that this will apply.

Gorse

When he was at college Daniel had a one-night stand with a stranger he met at a party. A few days later he realized he had caught something. He went to the doctor, who told him that he probably had genital herpes, and took a swab to send for testing. The results confirmed the diagnosis, and the doctor sent Daniel literature about genital herpes and how to manage it. But of all the sensible things the doctor told him the only thing he latched onto was the fact that it was incurable. He didn't bother to read the leaflets because there was no cure. He was deeply depressed for two months. Slowly he came round and got on with life, but he still despaired whenever the sores came back, which they did every six weeks or so.

Five years later he got engaged. He and his girlfriend Siobhan were always careful not to make love during a herpes attack, but he never went to get treatment. Siobhan had read magazine articles listing lifestyle changes that could cut down recurrence. They were simple, obvious things like drinking less alcohol and avoiding too many late nights and unnecessary stress. But all he ever said was that doctors could not cure herpes, so there was no point doing anything about it.

Remedy description

People in a Gorse state give up hope. They choose not to look for solutions, or accept the first negative comment they hear as the end of all hope. Sometimes other people will suggest ways through their problem, but they convince themselves that nothing will work. The element of self-will in their pessimism does not make it any the less painful for them, and they do not enjoy the gloomy view they take of life. To this extent at least the Gorse state is one of true despair.

Gorse can be thought of as the next stage on from Gentian, since the Gentian person will usually try again with a little encouragement. If a Gorse person can be induced to try something it will be against his better judgement, and even while making the attempt he will assure everyone that it is doomed. When ill, he may trace his illness back to some constitutional fault or inherited trait.

Gorse is made from the flowers of the common gorse bush *Ulex europaeus*. The flowers glow a deep, rich, vibrant yellow, and makers use the sun method to prepare them. For both reasons, and because of its effects, this remedy is sometimes called the sunshine remedy.

Case discussion

At first sight we might read Daniel's reaction as apathy, and select Wild Rose. The clue that Gorse is a better choice lies in his unhappiness. Wild Rose people will not feel especially upset about the way things are, and just accept what happens, but Gorse people feel despair at the thought that they can do nothing to improve their situation. Daniel might need other remedies as well, but until he works on his Gorse state it will be difficult to see them.

EXERCISES
Gentian and Gorse

> **A** Re-read Hannah's story, used as an example of a Gentian state. Describe the things she might do that afternoon, assuming of course that she has not taken Gentian.
>
> **B** Now imagine that Hannah needs Gorse instead of Gentian. What differences might there be in the way she behaves during the afternoon?
>
> **C** Brenda refuses to go on a diet, despite what the doctor says, because she will never be able to lose weight. She is big-boned and that's just the way things are. Does she need Gentian or Gorse – or Larch?

Sweet Chestnut

Doctors told Linda she had cancer when Oliver, her only child, was two years old. She had all the orthodox treatments, and many of the unorthodox as well. For a time she rallied and seemed to be on the mend, but two years after the first diagnosis her condition suddenly took a turn for the worse. Her weight dropped to four and a half stone. She refused to give in to the disease, and decided that whatever it cost she would see Oliver grow up. But the pain grew worse. The specialist prescribed morphine and said that there was nothing further he could do.

She lay in bed at home, cared for by her husband and a nurse who called in twice a day. She could hardly bear the pain and slowly sank into despair. She would have been glad to die if it had not been for Oliver, but she could no longer bear to have him in the room because he reminded her of what she was losing.

Remedy description

The negative Sweet Chestnut state includes deep, genuine anguish, total despair and the end of hope, and the certainty that all options have been explored without finding any way out of a situation. We often associate these emotions with crushing events such as serious illness, bereavement and miscarriage. Quieter, less dramatic triggers include redundancy, or despairing of ever forming a genuine relationship with someone. As with all the remedies, the key is the response to the situation rather than the situation itself, and what will cause a Gentian state in some will lead straight to Sweet Chestnut in others.

Sometimes we have trouble distinguishing Sweet Chestnut from Gorse, in that both have to do with a sense of hopelessness. The key difference lies in finding where the hopelessness originates. To some extent Gorse people choose hopelessness. They give up before looking. Sweet Chestnut people have hopelessness thrust upon them. They search for a solution but find nothing.

The Sweet Chestnut remedy is made from *Castanea sativa* and prepared using the boiling method. It helps to ease anguish and heartache so that we can take control again. Miracles might happen, but even when they do not we are able to face the future with renewed heart and make the most of the opportunities that remain.

Case discussion

Linda needs Sweet Chestnut – and given the extremity of her situation it would be difficult to look beyond this and Rescue Remedy. Sweet Chestnut could give her the strength to go beyond despair and say goodbye to Oliver in her own way, if that is what has to happen.

Oak

The hospital's radiography unit closed down and its work was transferred to a larger unit a few miles away. Everyone told Margaret she would never work again.

Margaret was 55. She refused to give in. Work was her main interest now that the children had all left home, and she made up her mind to find a new job. First she tried all her contacts at the hospital to see if she could arrange a transfer to another team. When she drew a blank she took to scouring the local papers for job opportunities, but the advertisers offered little beyond work stuffing envelopes and pyramid selling. Reluctantly – it was something other people did – she went along to the Jobcentre in the next town. The people there were very nice to her, and all sounded very positive. There were no suitable jobs at present, but they told her to call in as often as she could because something could come in any day and it might be just what she was looking for.

She called in every day for three months and nothing turned up. Eventually she went back to the local papers and answered one of the adverts. A man interviewed her over the telephone and after three minutes gave her the job. She was to phone people up, posing as a researcher, and ask ten questions about home improvements, with the aim of getting leads for a company that sold replacement windows. She would be paid commission on any orders, plus phone expenses.

It was a job of sorts, but not what Margaret wanted. She continued to visit the Jobcentre, kept an eye on the local papers, and spent every afternoon and evening clamped to the phone. One day she fell ill and could not get out of bed. As soon as she could sit up she picked up the phone and her list, and doggedly carried on where she had left off.

Remedy description

Oak people are steady and reliable, and often end up carrying other people's burdens as well as their own. They work with immense strength and at the same even pace, never resting, never hurrying, never showing how tired they are until they eventually collapse with exhaustion. As this shows, the indications for Oak are all positive. Problems begin when Oak people fail to see that they have lost a battle. They go on fighting when a retreat would do more good, and unnecessarily waste their strength. The remedy helps people in this state stand back and take stock, and at the same time reinforces their natural endurance. Oak is a restorative, then, and a lender of true perspective.

The Oak remedy comes from the pinhead-sized female flowers of the common oak, *Quercus robur*. These are prepared using the sun method.

Case discussion

Oak would help restore Margaret's great strength and patience and
help her get off the treadmill of her badly paid, unsuitable job.
Instead of working herself into the ground she could sit back for a
time and identify what she really wants out of life. This may mean
early retirement or a new start in a new career. Either way Oak will
give her the balance and strength she needs to carry her project
through.

Mustard

Fiona suffers from pre-menstrual tension. She experiences all the
classic symptoms, such as irritability, tiredness, poor self-image,
tension and headaches. Worst of all is the black depression that
sweeps over her once a month. Nothing will shift it, and it comes
regardless of what is happening in her life. In the past it has ruined
Christmas mornings and summer holidays and a friend's wedding,
all with equal and impartial finality.

Remedy description

People take Mustard to deal with feelings of hopelessness,
depression and despair that have not been caused by events in their
lives. In a Gorse state we can point to something wrong, such as an
illness or a misfiring career or marriage, but in a Mustard state
everything seems fine. People in a Mustard state can count their
blessings and see how all the things they have should make them
happy. They can't account for the way they feel.

The Mustard remedy helps lift the black clouds of gloom and gives
us a feeling of peace and joy. It is made from the yellow flowers of
the wayside plant *Sinapsis arvensis*, which are prepared using the
boiling method.

Case discussion

Should Fiona be given Gorse or Mustard for her depression? The
answer hinges on whether there is a reason for her feeling the way
she does. In one sense there is a reason – hormone levels and their
effect on emotions. But in Bach Flower Remedy terms there is no

reason, because she can't point to events in her life and give those as the cause for the way she feels. For this reason Mustard is the better choice.

Physical symptoms like headaches and tension do not in themselves indicate any remedies. But other symptoms Fiona feels are emotional, and for them we can suggest remedies: Impatiens or Beech for her irritability; Olive or Hornbeam for her tiredness; and Crab Apple for her poor self-image.

EXERCISES

Sweet Chestnut, Mustard and Oak

Which of the three remedies Sweet Chestnut, Mustard and Oak would you suggest to these people? (Hint: one person needs two remedies.)

A Candace has been diagnosed with glandular fever and told to have complete bed-rest. She continues to come into work every day at her regular time, and puts in her usual ten-hour day. It is her company and she doesn't want to let her staff and customers down. She looks very sick.

B Yesterday Terry's football club won the league title after a long and very hard season. There is a big celebration planned for tonight. He knows he should be looking forward to a great evening, but people keep telling him to cheer up because he looks and feels so depressed.

C Laura suffered serious injuries when the car her husband was driving crashed into a tree. While in hospital she keeps busy and forgets her own troubles by helping nurse her husband and another man in the same ward. Then, without warning, her husband picks up an infection during a minor operation and is dead within two days. Laura arranges the funeral and struggles through the burial service. Then she cracks and her despair is awful. She can see no way through.

Willow

Two days before her school's ski trip Helen catches the flu. Five other girls are also off school, and three of them, including Helen, are so ill that there is no question of them flying out on Friday night as planned. Helen blames the teachers for her illness because they made her play hockey in the rain.

Even after the crisis Helen remains under the weather, and says she doesn't feel any better. She grumbles all the time. Nothing pleases her. When one of her luckier friends calls up from Austria to ask how she is she does not ask any questions about the trip but just grumbles about how unfair the situation is – why should she be the one to suffer?

Things are no better when her friends get back. They want to share their experiences with Helen, but Helen calls their enthusiasm boasting and resents the fact that they have enjoyed themselves.

Remedy description

The Willow state combines self-pity, sulkiness and resentment. People in this state see life in the negative, feel bitter about other people's happiness, and make dull and wearisome company. Everything is someone else's fault. We all get like this from time to time – the trick is to get back to the positive as soon as possible, and that is what the Willow remedy helps us do. It puts our troubles in perspective. We realize that if we are going through a bad time it is not because of other people or a vindictive fate, but simply because we all go through bad times now and again. Back in balance, we are able to share and enjoy the triumphs of others in a generous and open way, and can laugh more when things go wrong in our own lives.

The Willow remedy is prepared using the boiling method. The tree used is the yellow osier, *Salix vitellina*.

Case discussion

There might be an argument for suggesting Chicory to Helen if she is exaggerating her suffering in order to get more attention from her friends and family, and some practitioners would consider Crab Apple to help cleanse the lingering mental effects of the flu. Whether or not these are appropriate, the mood remedy required is clearly Willow.

EXERCISES
Willow

A How might you expect Helen to react to the phone call if she had taken Willow earlier?

B Without looking back at the remedy description, write down four key words that you feel sum up a Willow state. Check your answer by re-reading the indications for Willow.

Other depression remedies

When we feel depressed, or say we are sad or unhappy, we can mean a number of different things. Here is how other remedies might be used to combat depression.

- Agrimony, if we hide our depression from ourselves and others by making a joke of our feelings.
- Chicory, if we feel unhappy because we are not getting the love and attention we feel we deserve.
- Crab Apple, if we feel depressed about the way we look.
- Elm, where we are brought down by the weight of responsibility on our shoulders.
- Honeysuckle, when we relive the past and feel saddened by our regrets.
- Pine, when unhappiness is linked to guilt.
- Star of Bethlehem, when we feel great sadness due to grief.

EXERCISES

Depression and hope

A married woman has had unprotected sex but is not pregnant. Supply more details of her situation, actions or feelings, assuming that she needs the following remedies.

A Gentian.

B Gorse.

C Sweet Chestnut.

D Oak.

E Mustard.

F Willow.

Recap

- Gentian is for a relatively mild sense of despondency when something has gone wrong and we feel like giving up.

- Gorse is a deeper form of depression, where we have given up hope and made up our minds that things will not improve.

- Sweet Chestnut helps when we are at the end of the road, and there really is no way out of our difficulties. The Sweet Chestnut state is a deeper despair than either Gentian or Gorse.

- Oak is for slow, steady, reliable people who never know when they are beaten.

- Mustard helps when we feel unhappy, gloomy and depressed but cannot see any reason in our lives to justify feeling that way.

- Willow is for self-pity and resentment. For the person in this state everything is someone else's fault.

Answers to exercises

Gentian and Gorse

A She might waste most of the afternoon sitting around feeling upset and wondering if she will be able to find a way forward, but eventually she will move on.

B She might get home and tell her husband that she has no chance of working in translation, and refuse to look into the subject any more.

C Gorse, as she has chosen to give up and sees the weight problem as insoluble in its essence. (Larch would apply if she felt the problem were insoluble only for her, due to her particular lack of will-power, but that other people in her position would be able to solve it.)

Sweet Chestnut, Mustard and Oak

A Oak.

B Mustard.

C Oak and Sweet Chestnut.

Willow

A She would talk less about her own plight and be more interested in the good time her friends were having.

B You could have chosen many words, for example bitterness, resentment, self-pity, grumbling, sulkiness, and unfairness.

Depression and hope

Here are some possible answers.

A She has just started trying for a baby and is disappointed as she thought she was pregnant.

B She has been trying to get pregnant for two years, and now feels that nothing more can be done.

C She is 45 years old and desperate for a child. She has had several years of IVF treatment and the specialist has advised her to give up. The thought that she might be pregnant this time was the only thing keeping her going.

D She has already been trying to get pregnant for two years, and is determined not to give up.

E She had a fling with an old flame at a party, and feels she should be delighted that she has got away with it. But still she feels down.

F Her friend got pregnant without even trying, yet she is still waiting. It's not fair!

6 THE REMEDIES: CONFIDENCE

Aims of this chapter

Feeling we will not be good at something, being reluctant to try new things, saying we are useless or at fault – we might describe any of these negative feelings as a lack of confidence. In this chapter we concentrate on remedies that can help with different confidence issues. All four of them come from Dr Bach's 'Despondency or Despair' category.

- Larch – for people who expect failure and do not try to succeed.
- Elm – helps people who feel that they have taken on more than they can cope with.
- Crab Apple – for people with a poor self-image, who condemn themselves for what they are.
- Pine – for those who blame themselves when things go wrong, and make themselves unhappy through guilt.

Larch

See Chapter 4 for the full indications for Larch, the remedy for feeling that we are going to fail because we are not as capable as other people. In this state we avoid challenges rather than face up to the possibility of failing – and sometimes we view possible success with just as much trepidation.

Some people feel comfortable in a Larch state. Certainty of failure excuses us from having to make an effort and cope with success. The remedy can help us leave the comfort zone – and the stagnation that goes with it – and take on the challenge of getting more out of life. It also contrasts well with the Elm state, in which confidence becomes an issue only after commitments have been made.

Elm

Sue works as a childminder. Her busiest day of the week is Thursday, when she has four children booked in all day, plus another who comes for two hours after school. Her quietest day is Tuesday, when she has a baby all day and a three-year-old after lunch. She also has three children of her own, aged 5, 3 and 18 months. The eldest has just started school.

The last week has been especially difficult. A gang of builders are adding a conservatory and cloakroom to the back of the house. She has to watch the children all the time because of the tools and cement and other child traps left lying around, and the builders are forever traipsing through the house from front to back and back again, leaving all the doors open on the way. Her three-year-old has already escaped twice, and once got as far as the main road before he was spotted.

On Wednesday night the eldest child is sick and next day has to stay off school. The baby doesn't seem well either and only stops screaming if she picks him up. Trying to get lunch ready for seven children at one o'clock, she realizes that the plumber has turned off the water so that he can fit a sink in the new cloakroom. She bursts into tears. She can't cope any more, and begins to feel very sorry for herself. Why should she have all this to deal with when other people just do as they please?

Remedy description

Larch people lack confidence in their abilities and so do not try things, but Elm people are extremely capable and quite willing to take on responsibility. In fact they have so much faith in themselves that they do not always know when to stop, and only when something goes wrong do they suddenly see how much they have taken on. Then comes a crisis of confidence, and they doubt their ability to fulfil their obligations. Indeed, they may wonder if anyone could cope with so much. Their feelings at these times range from tiredness and weariness through to depression and worry – but Elm people are naturally resilient, and with the help of the remedy they quickly recover their poise and self-belief.

Elm comes from the catkins of the common elm tree, *Ulmus procera*, which are prepared using the boiling method.

Case discussion

This is clearly not a case for Larch. Sue has enough confidence to take on an extremely difficult job and can cope one at a time with all of the challenges facing her. Problems only begin when there are too many challenges at one time. Elm will restore her usual level of confidence, and also help her see her limits better and cut down the pressure to a more reasonable level. She would also benefit from Willow, since a strong vein of self-pity and resentment creeps in at the end of the story.

EXERCISES

Larch and Elm

Your friend is chief buyer for a large toy shop. Christmas is coming and one of her main suppliers has let her down. She tells you she has lost her confidence.

    A Add details to this story to make it clear that the remedy your friend needs is Larch.

    B Now change the story so that she clearly needs to take Elm.

Crab Apple

At 17 years of age Adam has already made up his mind that he is a failure and will never get a girlfriend – he is too fat. His mother laughs it all off, saying he is only a few pounds overweight and will soon work it off if he takes some exercise, but every time he looks in the mirror he sees a grotesque image looking back at him. He hates himself and the way he looks.

His next-door neighbour Janet is 34 and married with no children. She is quite happy with the way she looks, when she stops to think about it – but stopping is something that she rarely does. Instead she is up every morning, well before her alarm clock rings, in order to clean the house from top to bottom before she goes to work. If she chances to get up late and miss her daily clean she finds it difficult to concentrate on her day job for thinking about how dirty the rugs will be and how badly the cushions will want plumping.

Remedy description

Often described as the cleansing remedy, Crab Apple has two main uses. One is for those times when we feel dirty or unattractive, as if something is wrong with us and needs to be removed. Often the thing we are concerned with is relatively unimportant, such as a spot or a minor chest infection, but we blow it up out of all proportion until it simply must be dealt with before anything else.

The second use relates to the first, and comes when any small detail in the world around us weighs too much with us. The man who lets the roast beef burn while he concentrates on adding just the right amount of thickener to the gravy needs Crab Apple, as does the woman who swoops down to wipe mud off her nice clean floor while her three-year-old screams with shock after falling over. This aspect of Crab Apple is often associated with over-fussy cleanliness and tidiness.

Crab Apple fussiness can shade into neurotic obsessions, and compulsive hand-washing is a Crab Apple condition, as is checking and re-checking that the gas is turned off, the cheque signed, or the house key in its usual pocket. Feelings of uncleanness can degenerate into disgust for the physical life, so that biological functions such as eating, making love and defecating feel unpleasant or disgusting.

As a cleanser Crab Apple purifies our feelings about ourselves and our surroundings. We can relax more and enjoy the basic, sensual experience of being alive. Our sense of true perspective returns and we can see and enjoy ourselves for what we really are.

The remedy Crab Apple is prepared using the boiling method and the pink-white flowers of the common crab apple tree, *Malus pumila*.

Case discussion

Adam and Janet both need Crab Apple. It will help Adam see beyond his weight problem, and Janet will be able to concentrate better on her job and resist the compulsion to clean every day. Adam could also benefit from Gorse, which would help him find hope again, and White Chestnut would help Janet control her wayward thoughts. But for both of them Crab Apple is the key remedy.

Pine

When Jenny was three months pregnant with her second daughter her husband left her for another woman. That was 15 years ago. Now Jenny's daughters are both doing badly at school. The youngest has been threatened with expulsion for bullying. The eldest, who is 17 and should be studying for exams, is due to appear in court charged with shoplifting and possession of heroin.

Jenny is at her wit's end with worry over both of them, but underneath the concern a nagging voice tells her that she, Jenny, deserves all she gets. She wrestles with this idea – she knows there is no basis for it – but it persists. It is her fault her husband left her, her fault her eldest daughter is using drugs and in trouble with the police, her fault that her youngest is off the rails and likely to have to change schools. It is all her fault.

Remedy description

People in a Pine state blame themselves when things go wrong. Sometimes someone else is at fault – but even where the Pine person really has done something bad the answer must be to learn from the experience, put the wrong right if possible, and then move on. Guilt is extremely destructive when it is not dealt with, and can poison lives.

Pine people often work hard, as if trying to make up for their failings, but never feel satisfied with what they have done. The remedy helps them move away from guilt and into a more positive frame of mind where they can judge themselves fairly, and be aware of their achievements as well as their failings.

The tree used to make the Pine remedy is the Scots pine, *Pinus sylvestris*, and it is prepared using the boiling method.

Case discussion

Jenny could benefit from several remedies. One obvious candidate is
Red Chestnut, for her anxiety over what will happen to her daughters,
and another is Star of Bethlehem, if she has not fully got over the shock
of her husband leaving her so suddenly. But Pine is the most important.
It will help her deal with the overwhelming feelings of guilt so that she
can look for rational solutions to her family's problems.

EXERCISES
Crab Apple and Pine
Which remedy out of Crab Apple and Pine would you suggest
for these mothers?

  A She says if her teenage son is late for school it is her
  fault. She would rather he be an hour late than have
  him go in looking dirty.
  B She says if her teenage son is late for school it is her
  fault. She ought to get him out of the bathroom
  earlier.

Other confidence remedies

We can easily see how Larch and Elm relate to confidence. With
Crab Apple and Pine the link is less obvious until we think about
how these states impact on the people living through them. Crab
Apple people may become so obsessed with controlling small
details that they feel insecure in the wider world. Or they may
dislike the way they look to such an extent that they avoid social
situations and feel ill-at-ease in company. As for Pine people, they
are always ready to take blame for everything that goes wrong, and
will condemn themselves for not doing better even when they have
achieved great things. They are always at the point of assuming
failure. Both states eat away at self-confidence and stop people
living full and enjoyable lives.

Many remedy states can present as confidence issues.

  ■ 'There are things in my life that I don't trust myself to
  face' could be an indication for Agrimony.

■ 'I'm not sure that I can stand up to him' could indicate Centaury.

■ 'I lack confidence when it comes to taking decisions' could indicate Cerato.

■ 'I'm not sure I can control my temper' could be an indication for Cherry Plum.

■ 'I'm not sure I can do anything about it' could indicate Gentian.

■ 'I have no confidence in the future' could indicate Honeysuckle.

■ 'I don't trust her to take care of herself' could indicate Red Chestnut or Chicory.

■ 'I'm not sure which to choose' could indicate Scleranthus.

■ 'I don't trust him to take decisions' could indicate Vine.

■ 'I'm not sure what I want to do with my life' could indicate Wild Oat.

EXERCISES

Confidence

Zara's glamorous friend Billie is desperate to be a model. They go to a fashion fair together, and to Zara's surprise a talent scout approaches her and not Billie. Supply more details of Zara's situation, actions or feelings, assuming that she needs the following remedies.

A Larch.

B Elm.

C Crab Apple.

D Pine.

Recap

■ Larch people fail to put sustained effort into achieving success. The remedy helps build up their sense of self-worth and self-belief.

- Elm helps temporary crises of confidence in people who are normally capable but have taken on too much.
- Crab Apple is for feeling contaminated or unclean, and helps people who dislike the way they look or the way they are.
- Pine helps people cope with guilt.

Answers to exercises

Larch and Elm

A The supplier was appointed by her earlier in the year, and she obviously did not do a good job in choosing them. Now she no longer thinks that she has what it takes to negotiate such important contracts, and is thinking of resigning to get out of the situation.

B She can find a new supplier, but it will take time, and with so much else to do and so few staff she doesn't think anybody would be able to cope in her position.

Crab Apple and Pine

A Crab Apple – she doesn't appear to feel guilty over her actions, so Pine is not indicated.

B Pine.

Confidence

Here are some possible answers.

A She refuses to give her name and address, because she is sure she couldn't cope with the job.

B She says yes to a contract but then remembers she has already got too much on, what with exams coming up and her part-time job. She begins to have doubts – will she be able to cope with all this at once?

C She refuses to give her name and address – she is too fat and ugly.

D She apologizes to Billie.

7 | THE REMEDIES: WHEN SOMETHING HAPPENS

Aims of this chapter

We will look at seven remedies in this chapter. Most are only ever used as mood remedies – and all are remedies you might reach for when something happens and you need help to deal with it.

- Rescue Remedy – the crisis or emergency remedy, and the flower remedy equivalent of a first-aid kit.
- Rock Rose – placed in the 'Fear' category by Dr Bach, who said it was for extreme fear and terror.
- Sweet Chestnut – a 'Despondency or Despair' remedy for great anguish and suffering.
- Star of Bethlehem – another from the 'Despondency or Despair' group, you can take this whenever you are suffering from the after-effects of a shock.
- Olive – a remedy from the 'Insufficient Interest' group, this is for exhaustion caused by suffering or hard work.
- Chestnut Bud – again from the 'Insufficient Interest' group, this is for people who fail to learn from experience.
- Walnut – classed among the remedies for those 'Over-sensitive to Influences and Ideas', this helps deal with change and outside influences.

Rescue Remedy

Tony and his wife Micki kept bees. Getting stung was an occupational hazard and on the whole they were used to it. Normally the bees were docile, but on this occasion – perhaps due to the threat of thunder – they were restive. Nevertheless the honey had to be removed before it set solid, so Tony armed himself with a bee suit plus two pairs of trousers, two sweaters, and two pairs of socks and gloves.

All was well for about ten minutes. Then the even hum rose to an angry buzz, and within seconds Tony was covered from head to foot in vengeful bees. He could feel them stinging him through all the layers of clothing, and a couple were buzzing around inside his veil. He realized things were out of hand. Quickly he reassembled the hive and set off down the road.

Usually bees leave off their attack once the threat has gone, but on this occasion they pursued Tony and Micki for half a mile before they gave up. It was a hot day, and what with the extra layers of clothing and the burning stings Tony was feeling pretty groggy by the time he got back to the house. He stripped off, his wife vacuuming up the dead bees, and could see angry red bands across his chest and middle, with the odd sting here and there over the rest of his body. The stings burned like fire, he was shaking and frightened, and his throat started to close up. He began to panic. As his wife was reaching for the phone to call the doctor he thought of Rescue Remedy.

Remedy description

For a full description of Rescue Remedy and its contents see Chapter 2.

Case discussion

The great advantage of Rescue Remedy is its convenience. It lies ready to hand when things go wrong, and gives immediate help for immediate problems. If there were leisure to make a selection Tony might choose Star of Bethlehem to help the shock of the bee stings, Clematis for the groggy feeling, Rock Rose for the terror of feeling his throat close up, and Cherry Plum for the panicky loss of self-control – but he did not have time to select and mix a treatment bottle and did not need to, as all these remedies are already in the Rescue Remedy combination. He took four drops in water and felt the panic subsiding as his throat became normal and the shaking died away.

You can use Rescue Remedy over an extended period without running any risk, but it will not deal with underlying imbalances. For that you need to use a personal mix of single remedies. So if you find yourself turning to Rescue Remedy over long periods try to step back and think about why you need rescuing so often. For example, if Tony had been someone who often got stung because he failed to do up his bee suit properly then he might have needed Chestnut Bud. Impatiens would have helped if he was often in too much of a hurry to take proper precautions.

People sometimes turn to Rescue Remedy when conventional treatment is failing. This is what happened to James at the end of 1997. He was admitted to a cardiac hospital, via Casualty, and underwent by-pass surgery. He made a speedy recovery but reacted violently to a drug and was re-admitted to hospital with an infection in the incision. He became extremely ill and was moved to intensive care. His blood sugar was so low it could not be measured and he was on ventilation and life support.

Doctors operated to close the original wound. When he regained consciousness James was disorientated and confused. He kept trying to get out of bed 'to get to the airport'. He was given various drugs and had to be restrained with his hands tied.

At this point his wife said that the side-effects of the drugs were making him worse, and asked the doctors to stop treatment and give Rescue Remedy instead. Within the space of two or three minutes the monitor showed his heart rate falling from 110 to 87, and his blood pressure dropped from 150 to 134. He calmed down and began to sleep peacefully.

Some hours later Rescue Remedy was repeated with the same results on the monitor. The physician in charge wrote on his chart that he should be given Rescue Remedy when required, and that the nursing staff should be instructed in its use, along with other homeopathic remedies for renal failure.

A Bach practitioner who had helped James in the past was telephoned for further advice. She suggested White Chestnut for his worrying and Vervain for the frustration – this was his type remedy. These were added, and within two weeks his confusion vanished completely and his kidneys were functioning normally. Soon after that he returned home.

Rescue Cream

Three-year-old Sebastian developed eczema around his mouth. The doctor said it was nothing to worry about. The problem was probably caused by his dribbling while he was asleep, the skin was still growing, and in a year or so things would improve. In the meantime he prescribed a mild steroid cream to keep the eczema under control. This suppressed the problem, but as soon as all the cream was gone the skin erupted worse than ever. The doctor confirmed his earlier diagnosis and prescribed another tube of the same cream.

Mindful of the possible side-effects of applying steroids to the skin, Sebastian's parents decided not to use the cream any more and instead went to the pharmacy to see if there was something safer. The chemist suggested trying Rescue Cream, saying it was probably the mildest cream they had. So they applied Rescue Cream morning and night for the next four days. The eczema vanished and did not return.

Remedy description

For a full description of Rescue Cream and its contents see Chapter 2.

Case discussion

Rescue Cream is the obvious choice for skin conditions and bumps and bruises. Nevertheless, some forms of skin problem – including some types of eczema – don't respond well to any cream, and may even get worse. An alternative approach would be to add the liquid remedies Crab Apple and Rescue Remedy to water and use this as part of a simple cleansing routine. Other remedies could be used instead, depending on the emotional state of the person being treated. This would be a back-up to normal oral use of the remedies.

Rock Rose and Sweet Chestnut

We introduced Rock Rose in Chapter 4, 'Fear and Worry', as the remedy for great fear and terror. Dr Bach described it as 'the remedy of emergency', a description more usually applied to Rescue Remedy, and not only is it one of the main ingredients in

Rescue Remedy but in many cases you will want to make a straight choice between the two. We have already suggested that in emergencies you are more likely to have Rescue Remedy to hand and that you may not have time to consider alternatives. But sometimes you do have time. For example, you might suffer from frequent panic attacks in crowded places. Would it be best to add Rock Rose to your treatment bottle, or stick with Rescue Remedy? And on what criteria should you base your decision?

The answer hinges on Rescue Remedy's role as an emergency remedy and nothing more. Rescue Remedy helps us over a crisis but does not address underlying issues. So we would use Rock Rose if we wanted to treat the panic attacks as an on-going underlying mental state – a long-term and recurrent terror of crowded places. But we would use Rescue Remedy if we were thinking of each attack separately, as one in a series of crisis situations. We mix treatment bottles to address chronic mental states, so almost by definition we will tend to use single remedies in mixes.

In the example given I would add Rock Rose to the treatment bottle, although I might carry a stock bottle of Rescue Remedy at the same time to get over any crises that come during the day – and that would mean any upset, not just the panic attacks. In fairness I should say that other practitioners might take a different view.

This chapter features another remedy that we have already seen: Sweet Chestnut, the remedy for absolute anguish and despair. We introduced this in Chapter 5, 'Depression and Hope'. People coping with the death of a partner or child often need Sweet Chestnut, and in this context it can be helpful to use it alongside Star of Bethlehem, the next remedy we will consider.

Star of Bethlehem

Judith worked as a travel agent. For years she suffered from recurrent cystitis. When this was at its worst she found it difficult to cope with the demands of her job. She was naturally a quick person, and tried to deal with clients quickly and efficiently. Sometimes she bullied her colleagues in order to get results, and she quickly lost her temper if computer or human errors got in her way.

At an initial consultation the practitioner suggested Judith take two remedies – Impatiens for her irritability, hurry and lack of patience, and Vine for her tendency to impose herself on other people without discussion. Judith took these remedies for three weeks and then came back for a follow-up consultation. She felt she had a little more patience, but that was the only change.

Nevertheless, at this consultation she talked for the first time about her only son, Robert, who had died four years before after developing Bright's disease. Her health problems had started then, and she put this down to the stress and pain she had gone through.

Remedy description

Star of Bethlehem is the remedy for shock and trauma. It is one of the most important ingredients in Rescue Remedy, where it helps us get over the shock of an immediate crisis. So we can take Star of Bethlehem to comfort bereavement, grief and loss, all of which represent a shock to the balanced person. But this remedy is for much more than immediate shocks.

We may try to deal with a traumatic event by repressing our feelings about it, bottling it up inside and carrying on as if nothing has happened. This will work for a time. But refusing to acknowledge a feeling is not the same as dealing with it, and in time the effects will be felt again, perhaps in an unexpected way. Whenever the shock occurred, or however deep the trauma is buried, Star of Bethlehem can help us assimilate it into our lives so that true healing can take place.

The Star of Bethlehem remedy is made from the white six-pointed stars of the flower *Ornithogalum umbellatum*. These are prepared using the boiling method.

Case discussion

The practitioner helping Judith did not identify the need for Star of Bethlehem right away, and quite correctly selected remedies for the emotions that were most apparent at the time. Although Impatiens and Vine did not seem to have very much effect, they did start the onion-peeling process and allow Judith to make the connection between her current problems and events in the past. With the help of Star of Bethlehem she began to process her grief. In fact, once Judith started talking about her son and his death she found her mind went back more and more to those old events. Honeysuckle was used to help her focus more on the present, alongside the Star of Bethlehem, and the response was so good that the cystitis also cleared up very quickly of its own accord, and six months later had not returned.

EXERCISES

Rescue Remedy, Rock Rose, Star of Bethlehem and Sweet Chestnut

For each situation select the one remedy that most applies out of Rescue Remedy, Rock Rose, Star of Bethlehem and Sweet Chestnut. Sometimes you might feel that more than one apply, but for the sake of the exercise choose only the most important.

A Ann's husband told her this morning that he is leaving her to live with a mutual friend, with whom he has been having an affair. He has packed and gone. She sits at the kitchen table too stunned to think.

B Following his wife's death Bob tried to keep things going for the sake of his two stepchildren, hers by a previous marriage. But there seems to be no light left and nothing to hope for. He has considered suicide, but then what would happen to Luke and Nancy?

C After seeing the specialist Tim sits in the car outside the hospital too scared to drive home and tell his wife the bad news. He is not even sure if he can say the name of the thing that will kill him in six months' time.

D Roy's parents divorced when he was three years old, and he went to live with an uncle who was a drunk and used to beat him and his aunt. Now he is 34 years old. He has a drink problem and his wife has left because of his growing violence.

E Eve has been suffering for more than six years from giddiness and blinding headaches. She cries herself to sleep sometimes, she is so frightened of what is happening to her, but refuses point blank to see a doctor in case her night terrors turn out to be true.

Olive

Annie is determined to get a first class degree, and equally sure that her course work in the first two and a half years has not been up to standard. So in her last months at university she works 16-hour days on her assignments and thesis, and on revision for final examinations. During the three weeks that the exams are on she sleeps four or five hours a night, her mind working constantly, and promises herself a month of partying once everything is over.

But when the exams finally end she feels so exhausted that she turns down invitations and tries to rest instead. Unfortunately her mind will not switch off. She is still in revision mode, and if she goes to bed early she lies in the dark planning essays and time-tabling revision. She is so tired she could weep, but she can't rest.

Remedy description

Olive is the mood remedy for tiredness that comes after an effort. The effort concerned can be physical, such as clearing snow or digging the garden or recovering from illness, but is just as likely to be mental or emotional – people worn out by studying or a messy divorce also need Olive.

Olive works to restore energy. This does not mean that it gives us an artificial boost like some kind of pep pill. Instead it recharges our batteries naturally. We may feel energized at once, or we may take a wider view of our lives and actions, and make time for genuine rest.

Case discussion

Olive is the clear choice for Annie's tiredness, which has been caused by lack of sleep and too much effort. And she is also in a White Chestnut state, which is why her mind revolves around exams even though they have finished.

She may also need other remedies for her personality. Perhaps she demands too much of herself, and pushes herself too hard, which could indicate Rock Water or Vervain. And if her parents' expectations are to blame then she might think about Centaury or Walnut to help her go her own way without interference. The need for further remedies, if any, would become clearer once the Olive and White Chestnut states had been addressed.

Chestnut Bud

Jack drives an open-top sports car. It cost him a lot of money, and he takes good care of it – except that he keeps forgetting to put the roof up when he parks it outside his house. Consequently he spends quite a lot of time mopping up rainwater.

Remedy description

Our lives present us with opportunities to learn from experience. We learn by noticing our mistakes and the mistakes and successes of other people. Sometimes, however, we have blind spots. We may have a relationship with an incompatible partner, and when it fails link up with a very similar person from a similar background. Or we may work in a job we hate, and move heaven and earth to move to a different company where we do much the same job. We repeat our mistakes, sometimes several times, before we begin to see a way out of them.

There are degrees of severity to the Chestnut Bud state. At its worst we fail to identify the pattern, and think each event in the series is a brand new experience. More often we fail to learn effectively. We appear to be conscious of what is going wrong but do not take the lesson to heart. We do nothing to avoid repeating a mistake, almost through carelessness and inattention.

The Chestnut Bud remedy gives us clarity and helps us see where we are going wrong. It is made from the same tree as the White Chestnut remedy – *Aesculus hippocastanum* – but the new sticky buds are used instead of the flowers, and preparation is by the boiling method.

Case discussion

Chestnut Bud will help Jack learn from his mistakes and avoid repeating them in the future. As is usually the case, this remedy is unlikely to be his type remedy – although we would need to know more about him to be certain of this.

Walnut

Jonathan's doctor has told him to drink less alcohol. At the moment he averages 12 units per day, and he should be drinking a maximum of 21 in a week. So he promises himself that once he has reached his weekly limit he will stop until the next week starts. He starts counting on a Saturday, when he drinks 18 units. Sunday evening he has a pint of strong cider, which takes him up to his 21-unit limit for the week. The next round he has a mineral water. But his mates all laugh so on the third round he has another cider. By the end of Sunday night he has drunk another 15 units.

On Monday he decides on a different approach. He will not drink until ten o'clock at night. That way he will have less time and will consume less. But after work someone suggests a quick drink. Everyone else is keen. He tags along so as not to seem stand-offish.

On Tuesday morning he wakes with a hangover and decides that he will have to stop completely. That evening he stays in so as to avoid temptation. He feels uncomfortable watching television without a drink in his hand, but resists the call of the off-licence until five minutes before they close. Then he hurries round to buy six cans of lager for one last binge.

Remedy description

Walnut protects against outside influences, such as other people's opinions and ideas, and the set of circumstances in which we find ourselves. When we know what we want to do and are trying to do it, but find outside influences making things more difficult, that is the time to take Walnut.

By extension Walnut also helps us deal with times of change, and with old ideas and associations that hold us back from successful change. In this connection Walnut is sometimes referred to as the link-breaker, because it severs those ties that keep us from moving forward. It can help at all times of growth and change, from cutting teeth and weaning to retirement and bereavement.

The Walnut remedy is made from the female catkins of *Juglans regia*, the walnut tree, which are prepared using the boiling method.

Case discussion

Walnut is a clear choice for Jonathan. It will help him change his habits and deal with the outside influences that are stopping him from changing, such as his friends' ideas and the association he makes between watching television and drinking. It will also help sever his links with alcohol, as the alcohol, or more specifically the habit of drinking every evening, can itself be thought of as an outside influence.

There are hints that he finds it hard to refuse invitations, so Centaury might also be helpful.

EXERCISES
Olive, Chestnut Bud and Walnut

A Look again at Jonathan's story. How might it be different if Jonathan needed Chestnut Bud instead of Walnut?

B Which of the following statements are most likely to indicate the need for Olive (there is more than one): 1) I'm tired of your stupidity; 2) I feel tired just thinking about it; 3) I've worn myself out; 4) I've been working too hard; 5) I've been concentrating too hard.

EXERCISES
When something happens

Jack nearly crashes his car on the motorway. Supply more details of his situation, actions or feelings, assuming that he needs the following remedies.

A Rescue Remedy.

B Rescue Cream.

C Rock Rose.

D Star of Bethlehem.

E Olive.

F Chestnut Bud.

G Walnut.

Recap

■ Rescue Remedy is for emergency use when there is no time to consider more precise remedy choices.

■ Rescue Cream is used for bruises, bumps, scratches and various types of external trauma.

■ Star of Bethlehem helps us cope with shock, loss and grief. It can be used for current emergencies, but also helps us resolve old traumas that may be causing problems in the present.

■ Olive gives rest and new energy to us when we have over-extended ourselves physically, emotionally or mentally.

■ Chestnut Bud helps us learn from our mistakes and those of other people, so that we do not need to repeat them.

■ Walnut is the link-breaking remedy, helpful at times of change and whenever we need protection against outside influences.

Answers to exercises

Rescue Remedy, Rock Rose, Star of Bethlehem and Sweet Chestnut

A The choice is between Star of Bethlehem and Rescue Remedy, and could be argued either way. Ann has clearly had a shock so that Star of Bethlehem is the main remedy needed. But at the same time this is a one-off crisis situation, so Rescue Remedy would apply, and is more likely to be in her handbag ready to take.

B Sweet Chestnut is the main remedy, as Bob is going through a period of deep and heartbreaking anguish and can see no way out.

C This case is similar to A, in that Rescue Remedy would be a credible alternative to the main remedy needed, which is Rock Rose. Tim should probably use Rescue first and then add Rock Rose to his treatment bottle.

D This would be a case for peeling the onion to discover what is underneath Roy's present state. However, there seems a pressing need even at this stage for Star of Bethlehem to help him over the childhood trauma he suffered.

E Rock Rose would apply here. Eve's fear is more than an everyday Mimulus state, and shows the paralysis of will that is often associated with Rock Rose.

Olive, Chestnut Bud and Walnut

A Jonathan might have made repeated attempts to follow one of his plans, and keep failing for the same reason. He may not see why he is failing.

B Statements 3, 4 and 5 indicate Olive. (1 indicates Beech and 2 indicates Hornbeam. These remedies are explored in later chapters.)

When something happens

Here are some suggested answers.

A He is shaking. He stops the car to give himself time to calm down.

B He runs the car off the hard shoulder and onto a grass verge, stopping with a bump that bangs his head on the roof of the car.

C Two other cars are less lucky, and hit the lorry head on. He and several other people stop, but he does not go to help, terrified at the thought of what he might see.

D His mind flashes back to a bad crash that he was in five years before, and he feels again the trauma he felt on that occasion.

E He fell asleep at the wheel on his way home from work.

F This is the third time this has happened in as many weeks, and he can't see what he is doing wrong.

G He was driving too fast in fog. He knew it was stupid but his passengers were egging him on.

8 | THE REMEDIES: RELATIONSHIPS

Aims of this chapter

Bach Flower Remedies can give us an insight into our personalities so that we can control and enjoy our relationships more effectively. This chapter concentrates on ten remedies that can help us relate better to other people.

- Water Violet – one of the three 'Loneliness' remedies, this is for cool, self-possessed, private people who sometimes feel isolated.
- Impatiens – the second 'Loneliness' remedy, for people who like to live quickly and avoid companions because they slow things down.
- Beech – one of the remedies for 'Over-care for Welfare of Others'. People in this state need help to see the value in different ways of life.
- Vervain – another 'Over-care' remedy, this time for life's enthusiasts and campaigners, who in a negative state may turn into fanatics.
- Holly – one of the remedies for those 'Over-sensitive to Influences and Ideas', this is for people who feel jealousy, suspicion or hatred.
- Rock Water – an 'Over-care' remedy, for those who strive to perfect themselves and hope to set an example to others.
- Vine – also in the 'Over-care' category, Vine is for strong leaders who may use force to get their own way.
- Chicory – again in the 'Over-care' category, this is for people who like to be the centre of their loved ones' attention.

- Heather – the third of Dr Bach's 'Loneliness' remedies, used to help talkative people who become wrapped up in their own lives.
- Centaury – an 'Over-sensitive' remedy that helps us draw boundaries so that other people can't dominate us.

Water Violet

Having retired from his job as head teacher of a small private school, widower James planned to divide his time between his garden and his study. Fate had other ideas. His youngest son, recently divorced, was posted to a war zone. Somebody had to look after his three children – aged 8, 10 and 14, and all girls – and their mother was not in a position to do so. James felt he had no choice but to take them in.

James was kind in an impersonal way. He might have dealt more effectively with boys – he was used to that at his old school – but he found it impossible to cope with females. They seemed to fight and argue in a different way, and he decided that it would be better not to get involved. So he retired to his study and only came down for mealtimes, which were provided by his live-in housekeeper.

After three weeks he came across the youngest girl crying on the stairs. He tried to find out what the matter was, but she called him a stuck-up snob and ran away. All three children began to avoid him. He wanted to get close to them so as to help them better, but did not know how to start.

Remedy description

Water Violet people like their own company. They are nature's aristocrats, graceful and self-possessed, but can appear arrogant and proud because they find it difficult to mix with others and deal with the rough and tumble of communal life. Most of the time they keep their troubles private, and do not get involved with other people's problems, although they will give advice if asked to and try to help if the need for help is clear. Made by the sun method from *Hottonia palustris*, Water Violet helps people like this open up to others. It is more often used as a type remedy than a mood remedy.

Case discussion

After taking Water Violet, James will still be a private person who loves his solitude and his own quiet pursuits, but he will be able to communicate better with his grandchildren. He and the children might also find Walnut useful, as this remedy would help all of them adjust to their changed circumstances.

Impatiens

Brigitte has been in three road accidents in the last 18 months. The first time was in a queue of cars waiting to cross a roundabout. She saw a break in the traffic and shot forwards. Unfortunately the driver in front had not seen the gap and she went straight into him.

The second time was on the orbital motorway around Paris. She was hurrying to get to a meeting, and went for a gap in the outside lane without looking. A van took off her left-hand wing mirror. Fortunately that was the only damage to her car, and the other driver didn't stop.

The third time was the silliest, because she had no reason to hurry. It was Sunday afternoon and she was on her way back home after having lunch at her parents' house. The person in front suddenly slowed to a near stop. Without thinking, Brigitte swung out to overtake – and then had to swing out further, into the parked cars on her left, to avoid a dog that had walked out into the road. Luckily nobody was hurt, but this time her car was a write-off.

Remedy description

Impatiens is the remedy for people who live life in a rush. They put themselves under pressure even when it isn't necessary, and delay irritates them. Often they prefer to work alone so as not to be held up, and if they are working in a team they are likely to do more than their fair share or take work away from others because that way they can go faster. We can all get into an Impatiens state when we are in a hurry and someone or something is holding us up. Think of the last time you were parked illegally and queuing at the Post Office: that is an Impatiens state.

The Impatiens remedy is made using the sun method and the paler flowers from *Impatiens glandulifera*.

Case discussion

Brigitte could probably use Chestnut Bud as she seems to be having trouble learning from experience, but the main remedy she needs is Impatiens. This would help her relax more and not drive herself (and her car) so hard. She could take time to enjoy life instead of rushing from one end of it to the other as if she could not get it over quickly enough.

EXERCISES
Water Violet and Impatiens

Here are the indications for three different remedies. Try to identify which is Impatiens and which Water Violet. What is the other remedy?

A May isolate themselves from others to avoid being held back. Dislike social occasions because they get in the way. Concentrated and explosive.

B May isolate themselves from others to avoid social occasions. Dislike being the centre of attention. Quiet and timid.

C May isolate themselves from others to avoid too much social contact. Dislike crowds because they prefer their own company or that of a few close friends. Quiet and self-reliant.

Beech

Vera works for a medium-sized firm that organizes promotions and special offers for other companies. She is a team leader, in charge of three full-time staff and a pool of part-timers. When the company allocates a project to Vera it leaves her to run it however she likes, as long as she meets all the deadlines. Vera earns a small bonus if she gets the job finished early.

Her current assignment is a special offer on the back of a breakfast cereal box. Customers have to send in ten box tops plus a cheque for £3.50, and in return they get a complete breakfast service, comprising a melamine bowl and plate, a knife, fork and spoon, and a mug, all emblazoned with the cereal maker's logo. Vera's full-time people check the number of box tops, make sure the cheque is for the right amount and put it in a pile to be banked, and enter the customer's name and address on a computer. Every day they print the previous day's entries onto address labels, and the part-timers label the pre-packed parcels, bundling them into large plastic sacks ready for collection.

Vera sets very high standards, but fails to inspire her people to meet them. Instead she criticizes. 'Stupid' is a word that comes easily to her lips – and she applies it to any scheme of work that differs from her own. She long ago decided that the most efficient way to do this kind of job is to have one person remove and count the box tops, a second remove the cheque and make sure it is filled in properly, and a third input the information. Unfortunately one of her team – Maxine – works more slowly than the other two. Vera has tried Maxine on each of the three tasks. In the first two positions she holds up the third, and as inputter she can't get information on the computer fast enough. So Vera puts her on box-top-counting – the easiest job – and criticizes her. This makes Maxine so flustered that she works even slower and holds up the other two even more.

The obvious answer (which has occurred to her team) is to have the fastest typist do the inputting while the two others both count box tops and check cheques. But Vera says this method is stupid – her method would be the best if only Maxine weren't so idiotically slow.

Remedy description

In a negative Beech state we condemn and criticize other people for not being like us. Our own ways are reasoned and reasonable, so why can't others see that? Are they stupid, or doing it on purpose just to irritate us? This sort of intolerance can develop into persecution and hatred, although more usually it takes the form of irritable outbursts about other people's idiocy.

Beech is the remedy to help us accept and value other people and their different approaches to life. Instead of criticizing we can put ourselves in other people's shoes and experience in our imagination what other lives are like. We are slower to condemn and quicker to praise. Even the most negative Beech types have the potential to show fine discrimination between ideas and values, and this remedy helps us realize this potential and not fall into the trap of facile condemnation.

Beech is prepared using the boiling method and flowers from the common beech *Fagus sylvatica*.

Case discussion

Vera's main concern appears to be time. If Maxine were quicker the job would go faster, and she condemns Maxine because she is not fast enough. The argument for Impatiens is weakened, however, if we think for a moment how someone in an Impatiens state would react in the same circumstances. She would be likely to send Maxine off to make the tea while she did the work herself. Or she would quickly and impetuously reorganize the team if she thought it would save time.

Vera doesn't display Impatiens reactions. Instead, she takes the time to criticize Maxine despite the fact that this only makes matters worse. This need to criticize combined with her lack of flexibility indicates Beech.

Vervain

Trudy is a first year arts student at a London university. She is a passionate vegetarian and animal-rights campaigner and has helped form a direct action group among the students. Her university is known to be the most left-wing in the city, and mainly attracts left-wing students. There are a few more conservative groups, however, especially on the science and business courses, and one of them invites a right-wing politician to give a speech at one of its meetings.

The university is in uproar, and the Student's Union holds a public meeting in the canteen. Trudy joins with the others in denouncing the MP's visit because he is known to be pro-hunting and in favour of animal experimentation. After a long debate, the Union win majority support for a resolution that deplores the visit of this speaker to the university, but at the same time recognizes that if they protest they will be portrayed in the papers as being opposed to free speech. Students are advised to make their feelings known by staying away from the university or, if they do come in, by greeting the visitor with silence.

Trudy argues at length against this resolution. After the meeting she and a few others talk long into the night about what they should do, and decide to treat it as a matter of principle. They make 'blood bombs' out of eggs injected with red food dye. When the MP arrives, complete with press photographers, they shower him with bloody eggs. Later he gives an impassioned and very successful press conference on the evils of fanaticism and the threat to free speech posed by animal-rights campaigners and left-wing students in general.

Remedy description

In a Vervain state we are fired with enthusiasm for something. We may want to tell everyone about it so that they will be as enthused as we are, or we may bury ourselves in a task and hardly notice the rest of the world, but whatever we do is done with enthusiasm and energy and a sense of purpose.

Vervains hate injustice, and will defend the rights of other people as quickly as they will defend their own – so the Vervain state is not necessarily negative. It becomes so when enthusiasm turns into over-enthusiasm. The happy, willing worker then turns into a workaholic, unable to switch off, sleepless with plans for tomorrow, and working every hour God sends. The passionate defender of justice and liberty turns into a fanatic, unable to understand or even listen to other points of view.

Vervain helps to turn the negative state back into its positive. The Vervain person does not lose her commitment and passion, but she can understand other points of view. This makes her a more effective campaigner.

The Vervain remedy is prepared from the tiny pale mauve flowers of *Verbena officinalis*. Preparation is by the sun method.

Case discussion

Trudy shows a number of classic Vervain indications. First there is her enthusiasm and commitment to a cause. Next there is her willingness to argue and discuss – she actually enjoys the debate, even though it is going against her, and when she steps outside the democratic process it is in the name of a principle and after further discussion. In fact her need to persuade other students is the key to selecting Vervain rather than Vine. Both Vervain and Vine people are strong and determined, but Vine people are more ruthless and do not mind about hearts and minds, as long as they get their own way.

Turning to her treatment of the MP, we can see Vervain fanaticism coming to the fore. At the same time the lines between Vervain, Vine and Beech begin to blur. Fanaticism, ruthlessness and intolerance all seem to have some part to play in her state of mind, so there could be arguments for using all three remedies, although Vervain remains the key to her personality.

EXERCISES
Impatiens, Beech and Vervain

Georgina is in her fifties. She never married, choosing instead to concentrate on her career as a teacher. Two years ago she took early retirement from her job at an exclusive private school in Boston.

Her main pastime since retirement has been charity work. She is very particular about which charities she gets involved in, and will only help what she calls 'deserving' causes. Recently she refused to support a housing charity because she felt the people being helped were idle and responsible for their own plight. She expresses her impatience over what she sees as misty-eyed romanticism in some of the people she meets at social functions.

Can you decide which out of Impatiens, Beech and Vervain would be the best remedy for Georgina?

Holly

Vanessa is 63 years old and has been married to John for nearly 40 years. A few weeks ago they went to John's retirement party, which was held in a hotel. During the evening Vanessa met many of John's work colleagues for the first time. Several people, including John, had rather too much to drink. Vanessa didn't drink as she was driving.

Towards the end of the evening she lost sight of John. It crossed her mind that he might have made himself sick with drink, so she went outside to look for him in the garden. She walked around to the front of the hotel and saw him standing in a doorway by some stairs. He had his back to her and at first she thought he was alone and wondered what he might be doing. As she got closer, though, she realized that he was with a woman, someone wearing a black and silver dress, who she remembered seeing at the bar earlier in the evening. Not knowing what to do she stayed where she was. After a few moments the woman went back into the hotel – was she staying the night there? – and John turned and wandered off around the building. He didn't notice her.

Vanessa hasn't said anything to John about what she saw, but it is in her mind all the time. She finds herself looking through his post and racing to get to the phone first. She is deeply suspicious if he goes off by himself for more than a few minutes, and finds ways of getting her own back – small, spiteful things like throwing away books and changing the radio channel to one she knows he dislikes. And questions go around in her head. Was John seeing the woman back to her hotel room, or was he just leaving it? Had they slept together? How long had it been going on? And was this the first time that he had been unfaithful? As her suspicion grows she starts to pick fights with him just to have an excuse to scream and throw things. She wants to hurt him the way he hurt her.

Remedy description

Holly balances strong negative feeling directed at someone else, such as hatred, jealousy and spitefulness. When we deliberately hurt other people so as to get revenge and make them suffer that is a Holly state. Hatred and jealousy are not attractive emotions, and we may hide our hatred by calling it something else. Nevertheless Holly reflects a basic human emotion. We have all been in a Holly state at one time or another, and accepting how we feel is the first step to changing it.

Many authors describe Holly as the remedy for anger. Certainly Holly feels hot and burns bright, and anger can be built on hatred and jealously. But we can get angry for other reasons too, such as loss of control, impatience and intolerance, and in these situations other remedies would be indicated.

Holly works to support our innate ability to understand and forgive wrongs done to us. We can see the good in others and return good for evil. The remedy is made from *Ilex aquifolium*, the familiar holly bush associated with Christmas and notions of love and redemption. Preparation is by the boiling method.

Case discussion

Vanessa's state of mind centres on her suspicion and her need to lash out and get her own back. Her aim in taking remedies would not be to calm herself down to the point that she would accept the situation and carry on as if nothing had happened. Instead she would hope to step outside the negative desire for revenge and find a better way of sorting things out. So far she has not told John what she saw, so he has no idea why she is upset with him. Maybe he can't remember his drunken behaviour. Maybe he has always been faithful. Holly will help Vanessa approach the situation positively and take action to discover and resolve the real situation, rather than acting on suspicion and making things worse.

A useful helper remedy would be White Chestnut to help calm the constant nagging thoughts about what has happened. Some people might consider Cherry Plum as there is violence involved and she is losing her temper – but the Cherry Plum state is one of loss of control, when we feel we might hurt someone in spite of ourselves, and it is above all a fear remedy. Vanessa is working up to her rages quite purposefully, and using them as a tool to get revenge. She is not afraid of losing control, so Cherry Plum does not apply.

EXERCISES

Holly

Here are indications for three different remedies. Try to identify which one is Holly. What are the other two?

    A They grumble about the ill-deserved successes of other people. They are resentful and bitter.

    B They quickly become angry when a principle has been broken and an injustice done. Sometimes their beliefs drive them to extreme actions.

    C They believe that other people are acting against them, and want to get their own back. They may be spiteful and want to hurt people.

Rock Water

Alison has four children, aged seven, five, four and one. Her husband has a good job and they could afford to get outside help. Yet Alison does all the housework herself and refuses to hire a nanny or an au pair. The children are her job, and if she has to work harder then so be it. Every day she follows a strict timetable so as to get the children to their different activities on time – from recorder and piano lessons for the eldest to mother and baby groups for the smallest. And there is no self-pity in her. She is her own hardest critic when things go wrong.

Remedy description

The key to the Rock Water personality is the drive for self-perfection. She demands high standards of herself, sometimes impossibly high, and forces herself to follow rules and meet targets. When she fails she is dissatisfied and may punish herself by setting even higher targets for the following day. A story about the great Indian leader Mahatma Gandhi tells how he would sleep in the same bed as young women as a test of his ability to transcend desire. This is a typical Rock Water demonstration of self-sacrifice and self-control.

Rock Water traits include extremes in diet and exercise, punishing work schedules and spiritual activities that demand excessive self-denial. They will deny themselves the occasional treat such as a bar of chocolate or an extra glass of wine. Having set limits, they refuse to go beyond them, and in a negative state the emphasis on self-control is symptomatic of an over-concentration on self. This makes real spiritual development, in which the self is transcended, more difficult. Another part of the Rock Water personality that makes development difficult is their rigidity of outlook. Their view of the world may become so fossilized that they are unable to appreciate other and better insights.

Rock Water people do not try to persuade others to do as they do, in the way that Vervain people do, nor do they issue orders or criticize, as is the wont of Vine and Beech personalities. Instead they set an example, the implication being that this is the right way and that others may if they wish follow the same path.

The Rock Water remedy is unusual in that it is the only flower remedy that does not use flowers. Instead the mother tincture is water taken from a natural unspoilt healing spring and prepared using the sun method.

Case discussion

Alison's enthusiasm and energy might suggest Vervain, and her desire to look after her children all by herself might indicate Chicory. But Rock Water would be preferred over both. Look for example at her attitude when things go wrong. Vervain people would put the blame where it lay, and not assume that they have failed unless they really had, while Chicory people would tend to blame other people. And when Alison refuses help with the children it is in the name of duty more than love. She almost welcomes the chance to sacrifice her own needs and desires.

Vine

Martha is a freelance artist. A publisher commissions her to illustrate a children's picture book written by an inexperienced author. The publisher has used Martha before, and trusts her more than the author. So although the book will be based on the author's first draft he has told Martha to see that it doesn't go too far off the rails.

Martha is a strong character, and a good leader – but the author, whose name is Anna, seems to bring out the worst in her. Anna is quiet and it is difficult to get any opinion out of her at all. Martha quickly abandons any thought of persuading Anna to do things her way, and instead assumes compliance and goes ahead.

When the project is finished and delivered to the publisher it is rejected. Most of the quirky story ideas that got the publisher interested in the first place are no longer there. Instead there is a rather stately, staid book – beautifully illustrated, but dull. The publisher holds a meeting with Martha and Anna to discuss what has gone wrong, and much to her surprise Martha finds the blame put on her and her bullying.

Remedy description

Made using the sun method from the flowers of the grape vine *Vitis vinifera*, Vine is for people who know their own minds and assume that they know what is best for other people as well. They are wonderful leaders in an emergency, but they have a ruthless streak. If they can get where they want to go without having to explain or justify then they will, and they will use force to overcome any resistance. At their worst they are out-and-out bullies.

The remedy encourages the natural leadership qualities of Vine people into positive channels, so that they can guide rather than dictate. They can value the contributions of other people, listen to their ideas, and allow them to steer their own paths without interfering.

Case discussion

The Martha/Anna relationship was always likely to bring out the worst in both of them. Anna – as far as we could say without more information – is perhaps in a Centaury, Mimulus, or Clematis state, and will not easily stand up to a go-ahead, decisive Vine. Faced with a compliant partner with no apparent opinions the temptation to assume control proved too great for Martha. She fell into a negative

Vine state, and that is the remedy she needs to help her stand back and allow Anna the freedom to develop her ideas in her own way.

Chicory

David and his wife Jean have three children, all boys. David's great passion is football. Ever since they were little he has taken his sons to every home game that Leeds United play. He also got involved with the local youth teams and, thanks in part to his dedicated coaching, all the boys turned out to be useful players.

His eldest son Lewis is now 16 and going to a college, where he has met his first serious girlfriend. She isn't especially interested in sport, and Lewis seems more interested in her than in football. He says he wants to go to university and be a software designer after he graduates, but David has let it be known that he thinks Lewis is making a fool of himself. If he put in a bit of extra effort now instead of mooching around after that girl then he might get a trial with a professional team. He, David, has put a lot into getting Lewis this far, and he has had little thanks for all the sacrifices he made. He feels hurt and upset. He could accept his son giving up football, but he can't accept that he is no longer involved in his life.

Remedy description

The Chicory remedy is made using the sun method and the beautiful blue flowers of *Chicorium intybus*. This plant has a long tap root that digs deep down into the soil and is very difficult to dislodge – and this characteristic of the plant gives a clue to the remedy description, for Chicory people hold on to the people they love and do not easily let go. They need to be needed. In their positive aspect they have a great deal of love to give, but the negative side of this is that they expect love, duty and attention in return. If they do not get them in sufficient quantities they can become manipulative and may exaggerate their unhappiness and sense of loneliness and abandonment as a way of getting what they want.

The Chicory remedy helps to accentuate the positive, generous, giving side of Chicory people. Love can be given selflessly and without thought of return. And as a mood remedy Chicory can help all of us when we get into a possessive frame of mind and start to think about our relationships in terms of how important we are to the people we love, rather than thinking of what we can do for them.

Case discussion

David has been and is a wonderful father, full of enthusiasm and keen to be involved. Quite without his realizing it, however, involvement has been on his terms, and his enthusiasm conditional on getting back from his sons all the affection that he puts into them. As his sons grow up and grow away from him he no longer gets the recognition he wants. This hurts, and without the help of the Chicory remedy he may resort to emotional blackmail in order to keep control.

Walnut would also be useful for David, as he is going through a period of change and is having trouble adjusting.

EXERCISES
Rock Water, Vine and Chicory

Here is a list of key words. Which ones apply to Vine, which to Rock Water and which to Chicory? Note that some words belong to more than one of these remedies.

Aggressive, Authoritarian, Convinced, Cruel, Determined, Dictatorial, Disciplined, Domineering, Forceful, Hard-working, Idealistic, Inflexible, Interfering, Irritable, Joyless, Manipulative, Possessive, Rigid, Selfish, Sensitive, Tearful.

Heather

The doctor sees Ken's name on the appointment list and sighs. His sympathy dried up six months after Ken's wife died because of Ken's absolute inability to listen to any of the good advice and suggestions that he, the doctor, made. Bereavement counselling, a holiday, hobbies – whatever he suggested flew past Ken's ears and out the door, while Ken went on talking about all the things that had happened to him since his wife died.

As for Ken, he sits alone in the waiting room, suffering more vague aches and pains. He has never felt so isolated. Anna used to listen, and he used to have other friends as well, but since she died his friends seem to be avoiding him – and just at the moment that he so much wants to unburden himself. If only people would listen.

Remedy description

Heather people have a deep need to be listened to. They dislike loneliness and do anything they can to avoid it, and in a negative state become so self-obsessed that they talk about nothing except themselves and their concerns. Either they do not hear what other people say, or they seize every opportunity to turn the conversation back onto them. Dr Bach used to describe them as 'buttonholers' from the way they would seize hold of their listeners to stop them getting away. In extreme cases they will follow people down the road, seemingly not noticing that their company is not wanted. This drains the people they talk to, and as a result they soon find that people begin to avoid meeting them. The result is loneliness – the very thing they feared.

Heather people often have suffered, and genuinely do have tales of woe to tell, but forget that others have suffered too. The remedy can help them see beyond their own troubles. They can listen to and sympathize with other people, and this in turn makes them more sympathetic company.

Calluna vulgaris is used to make the Heather remedy. Preparation is by the sun method.

Case discussion

Sometimes people who have been bereaved find it difficult to move on. They may talk about the old days with their partners and live more in the past than in the present. This is a Honeysuckle state. Ken's condition is rather different. He certainly misses his wife terribly, and Star of Bethlehem may be indicated for that sense of loss and grief. But he is not reliving the past in a Honeysuckle way. Rather he is trying to communicate his present distress and the reason for it. He is not doing this well, and his inability to listen as well as talk is driving people away. For this reason the remedy most clearly indicated is Heather.

Centaury

For five years Clarissa has worked in a shoe shop. She has three co-workers – two other shop assistants, and the manager. There was never any friction under the old manager, but a few months ago he took a job in a bigger branch and the company sent in a temporary replacement, whose name is Evelyn.

Evelyn hasn't been with the company long, and has just completed her probationary period. She lives very near the shop. Within a week of her arrival she begins to take longer breaks while she goes home on various errands. At first she asks each of her assistants in turn to cover for her, but the other two soon object. Clarissa always says yes, so she ends up doing all the covering. She takes messages for Evelyn, goes to the bank for her and deals with customer problems.

After a few weeks Evelyn says that as Clarissa is doing the banking she might as well take over the daily accounting as well – it will be good training for her. Clarissa doesn't say anything, and from then on she stays behind every evening to do the books. Evelyn gives her the keys so that she can lock up when she has finished.

Remedy description

Centaury people are willing helpers. They like to be useful, and get pleasure from assisting friends and relatives. They like to say 'yes' but often find it difficult to say 'no'. When more forceful and demanding people latch onto them they turn from willing helpers into servants and slaves.

Centaury is the remedy to help people caught in this kind of trap. It doesn't turn people into ogres or make them tyrants – they will always be kind and gentle and willing to help. But it does allow them to stand up for themselves when they are in danger of being exploited, and draw boundaries between their own needs and those of other people.

The Centaury remedy is made from the small, pink, star-shaped flowers of *Centaurium umbellatum*, which are prepared using the sun method.

Case discussion

Some might argue for Walnut, the remedy to protect against outside influences, but Clarissa is not really unsettled by Evelyn's ideas and opinions. She simply needs to draw a boundary between what is a reasonable request for help and what is an unfair imposition. The remedy that can help her say 'no' is Centaury. It will help her take a stand and refuse to do her manager's job for her.

EXERCISES

Heather and Centaury

Here are indications for three different remedies. Try to identify Heather and Centaury. What do you think the other remedy is?

A Other people find it hard to say 'no' to him. Good at being the centre of his family's affections, and enjoys knowing all about their doings, but gets very upset if he feels slighted.

B Finds it hard to get other people to listen. Dislikes being alone. Self-obsessed with little interest in other people's affairs.

C Finds it hard to say 'no' to others and tends to be the submissive one in relationships.

Other relationship remedies

Other remedies introduced in previous chapters could be classed as 'relationship' remedies. Here are some examples.

■ Mimulus would help shy people whose anxiety makes them avoid social situations.

■ Red Chestnut helps those who worry over the welfare of other people.

■ Agrimony helps those happy, sociable people who use company to avoid facing up to their hidden problems.

■ Walnut helps where other people's ideas and opinions influence us away from our own path.

EXERCISES

Relationships

Guy edits a newspaper that has just been bought by a millionaire businessman. The new owner wants to be more involved in the editorial side. Supply more details of Guy's situation, actions or feelings, assuming that he needs the following remedies.

    A Water Violet.

    B Impatiens.

    C Beech.

    D Vervain.

    E Holly.

    F Rock Water.

    G Vine.

    H Chicory.

    I Heather.

    J Centaury.

Recap

■ Water Violet helps when we feel aloof and cut off from other people. Water Violet types are self-sufficient and enjoy their own company, but can suffer through appearing proud and unapproachable.

■ Impatiens is for impatience, and especially for people who are always in a hurry.

■ Beech helps us to see the good in other people, so that we are not too quick to criticize.

■ Vervain helps us when our enthusiasm goes too far, so that we drive ourselves too hard or become fanatical and unable to listen.

■ Holly drives out strong negative emotions that are directed at other people, especially hatred, spite, envy and suspicion.

■ Rock Water brings flexibility and a sense of proportion when we deny ourselves pleasure in the pursuit of some ideal.

■ Vine is the remedy of leadership. It brings out the best in strong, decisive people who at times dominate through force instead of persuasion.

■ Chicory helps us to love freely and not ask for anything in return. It helps when we feel the need to control or possess or dominate the people we love.

■ Heather gives us a sense of perspective on our own troubles, so that we can see them in relation to other people's needs. It calms our garrulous self-obsession so that we can begin to listen.

■ Centaury helps us set limits. We can help without being dominated, and say 'no' when necessary.

Answers to exercises

Water Violet and Impatiens

    A Impatiens.
    B Mimulus.
    C Water Violet.

Impatiens, Beech and Vervain

Georgina's work for charity and career in education might suggest Vervain, and the mention of 'impatience' could suggest Impatiens. But the remedy indicated is Beech, since she seems more concerned with judging others than with helping them.

Holly

    A Willow.
    B Vervain.
    C Holly.

Rock Water, Vine and Chicory

Some of these could be argued differently depending on how you define the words, but your choice should not differ too much from this.

Vine: Aggressive, Authoritarian, Convinced, Cruel, Determined, Dictatorial, Domineering, Forceful, Inflexible, Rigid, Selfish.

Rock Water: Convinced, Determined, Disciplined, Hard-working, Idealistic, Inflexible, Joyless, Rigid.

Chicory: Convinced, Forceful, Hard-working, Interfering, Irritable, Manipulative, Possessive, Selfish, Sensitive, Tearful.

Heather and Centaury

> **A** Chicory.
> **B** Heather.
> **C** Centaury.

Relationships

Here are some suggested answers.

> **A** He may feel uncomfortable at having his space invaded, withdraw into his own office, avoid meetings, and stand on his dignity.
>
> **B** He may dislike having to discuss decisions with the owner as it slows things down. He may become irritable or agree to a wrong decision just to get a meeting over with.
>
> **C** He may criticize the owner's way of doing things, either to his face or behind his back.
>
> **D** He may object to the owner's involvement as a matter of general principle and threaten to resign.
>
> **E** He may envy the owner's power, and decide to get his own back in some way.
>
> **F** He may seek to demonstrate by his actions that he remains independent editorially. He may make a point of working longer hours and being better briefed than the owner.

G He may have an open battle of wills with the owner, and seek to dominate the relationship by sheer force of personality.

H He may feel threatened and try to keep a tighter hold on 'his' people so as to stay at the centre. He may take more interest than usual in the smallest decisions, and use deceit to score points against the owner.

I He may talk the situation out with anyone who will listen, and become wrapped up in discussing the impact on him personally rather than the more important impact on the paper's reputation.

J He may find it hard to resist the owner's point of view, and end up as a yes-man.

9 THE REMEDIES: ACTION AND INACTION

Aims of this chapter

This chapter focuses on 11 remedies that can help us take decisions and act upon them.

- Walnut – listed among the remedies for those 'Over-sensitive to Influences and Ideas', Walnut helps us move ahead on our own path.
- Olive – classed in the 'Insufficient Interest' group, Olive is for tiredness after action has been taken.
- Hornbeam – included in the 'Uncertainty' category, this helps overcome lethargy that comes at the thought of doing something.
- Cerato – another 'Uncertainty' remedy, this time for when we doubt our judgement.
- Scleranthus – a third 'Uncertainty' remedy, this helps us make decisions.
- Wild Oat – a fourth 'Uncertainty' remedy, for when we do not know what path we want to follow in life.
- Clematis – included in the 'Insufficient Interest' category, Clematis helps ground us when we daydream instead of acting.
- Honeysuckle – another 'Insufficient Interest' remedy, taken when we live in the past and not in the present.
- Gorse – also in the 'Uncertainty' group, this is for when we give up hope.
- Larch – a 'Despondency or Despair' remedy for when we lack the confidence to take chances.
- Wild Rose – grouped under 'Insufficient Interest', this helps dissolve apathy and lack of interest in life.

Olive

We looked at Olive in Chapter 7, 'When Something Happens'. It is the remedy for the kind of fatigue that comes after some effort has been made, and contrasts with another form of tiredness, one associated with the Hornbeam remedy.

Hornbeam

Janet has three young children, all under six. Looking after them takes all her energy, and by the time her husband Kevin gets home in the evening she is too tired to do anything but sit and watch television. Her parents are both dead, and Kevin's mother, a widow, lives several hundred miles away and is too frail to look after the children by herself. Their only other close relative is her brother, who is unmarried and lives abroad. As a result Janet hardly ever gets time to herself away from the children, and little jobs like balancing her bank account and sewing buttons on clothes do not get done. Other more enjoyable projects have been left too long as well: sorting out the garden, shopping for clothes, a swim at the local pools.

Janet and Kevin agree that Kevin will take a few days off work and take the children off to his mother's for a couple of nights. At last the great day dawns, and after a frenetic hour packing the car with children and supplies her family disappears up the lane and Janet is alone.

She has made a list of jobs she wants to get done, but first she sits down and has a cup of coffee. She puts away a few toys, finishing off a jigsaw that her eldest left on the table after breakfast. Then she picks up the TV remote control and almost without thinking switches on a daytime discussion show. She reads a couple of features in a magazine then looks at her list again, but cannot find the enthusiasm or energy to get started. Instead she makes another cup of coffee. By the time she has drunk that it is already past midday, so she makes a sandwich for lunch.

Remedy description

We are all familiar with the Hornbeam state. It comes when we look at the work we have to do and feel a wave of tiredness come over us. How will we find the strength to do with this? Where is the energy needed to get started? We put off the task, and instead fill in time with other and more meaningless activities.

The Hornbeam type of tiredness is all in the mind. If something exciting happens we immediately find our strength returns. Indeed, Hornbeam tiredness often (although not always) comes after we have had a good night's rest or have been on a break. This is why it is often referred to as the Monday morning feeling.

To compare the Hornbeam and Olive states, think about someone recovering from an illness. If the recovery has been long and hard and has left the invalid weak, that is an Olive tiredness. If the person is fully restored to health and energy but still has difficulty getting back to work, that is a Hornbeam state.

The remedy, which is made using the boiling method and the catkins from *Carpinus betulus*, helps to give us the impetus needed to begin a task. Once we have begun, the Hornbeam fatigue drops away of its own accord.

Case discussion

The children keep Janet busy, and she is often in an Olive state by the end of the day. At the moment, though, she has had a night's sleep and is not physically tired, only finding it hard to get started on what she wants to do. Hornbeam will bring her energy back into focus so that she can get the most out of her three days without children instead of frittering it away on television and jigsaw puzzles.

EXERCISES

Olive and Hornbeam

Select Olive or Hornbeam for these people.

> **A** Luke's body is fighting an illness, which has left him exhausted.
>
> **B** The in-tray seems mountainous at first but melts away once Joy starts on it.
>
> **C** Ray has recovered after his illness, and is struggling to pick up where he left off.
>
> **D** Dave can't enjoy his work at the moment – too many late nights have worn him down.

Walnut

We looked at Walnut in Chapter 7, 'When Something Happens'. Walnut helps us cope with change. It protects against outside influence, helping us move ahead on our own path regardless of what other people think. As such it can be compared with Cerato, another remedy for people who have to deal with other people's opinions.

Cerato

Bobbie is 21 and has started a new job, her first since leaving university, working in the PR office of a well-known dress designer. At the same time she has moved out of the family home and into a flat in a shared house. The house has a big garden.

Ever since she was a little girl Bobbie has wanted a cat. Her father is allergic to cats, so this is the first opportunity she has had to get one. There are four other people in the house. Two of them already have cats so she doesn't think her flatmates will object. She has the spare cash and the room – but every time she makes up her mind she wonders if she is doing the right and responsible thing. Will the other cats bully the new kitten? What if someone leaves the door open and it gets out before it knows its way around, and gets lost? What if she has to go to Paris or Milan next year for a fashion show – a strong possibility if she gets through her probation period? She becomes a bit of a bore on the subject of cat care. What does her mum think? What about her flatmates? And does the lady at the cat shelter think she is doing the right thing? This last gives her good advice – if you're not sure now, wait until you are. But it feels to Bobbie that she never will be sure, although inside she really wants the cat. She just wants someone to tell her it's the right thing to do.

Remedy description

Cerato people are capable of making decisions, but do not always trust their judgement. So they pause before doing what they want to do and seek reassurance from the people around them. They tend to be talkative about the one subject they need help with – 'What would you do in my place?' they ask over and over – and everyone they ask has a different opinion, which leaves them confused and no longer sure what to think. Under the temporary influence of someone else's point of view they sometimes do the opposite of what they planned. They may even attach themselves to people with very definite opinions and adopt their mannerisms and views.

The Cerato remedy helps put people like this back in touch with their intuition, which allows them to act more spontaneously and with more freedom. It is made from the intense blue flowers of *Ceratostigma willmottiana*, which are prepared using the sun method. Cerato is the only cultivated plant used in making the remedies – it comes from the Himalayas and does not grow wild in the British Isles.

Case discussion

If Bobbie had been acting on her decision while other people were offering their advice and causing doubt, then Walnut would have applied. If she had been unable to make up her mind in the first place, or were silently turning over the options in her mind, then Scleranthus would be the right remedy. As it is, Cerato is the only remedy indicated.

Bobbie is probably not a Cerato type, as she seems to have acted on a number of important decisions – about her university course, and about her new job and flat – on her own and with no fuss. But she is certainly in a Cerato state over whether or not to get a cat. This remedy will give her the self-belief to do what she knows she wants to do.

Wild Oat

The only thing that Nick was certain of when he left school was that he wanted to make a difference. He started a three-year degree course in sociology, but two months into the course he quit because it did not feel right. Instead he got a job working for a PR company, and was enthusiastic about it for a time. But he spent most of his days trying to place stories in local newsletters and minority cable TV channels. He left after six months.

Over the next ten years his restlessness continued. He spent six months training to manage a supermarket, nine months on a building site, and two years doing office work for a government department. He drifted into unemployment and tried to write a novel, but gave it up because he lacked belief in the characters and felt he had nothing worth saying. His thirtieth birthday was getting nearer and he still had not settled on the way he wanted his life to go.

Remedy description

Wild Oat people have a real desire to do something worthwhile – politically, socially, or in terms of their personal growth – but they do not have a clear idea of what that something should be. Consequently they drift from job to job, career to career, and hobby to hobby, never finding anything that meets their vague criteria. This leads to frustration and unhappiness.

The Wild Oat remedy helps people like this know their own minds and define their goal in life. It is prepared using the sun method from the wild grass *Bromus ramosus*. Despite the remedy's name, the plant used to make Wild Oat is not related to the oat family.

Case discussion

After taking Wild Oat for a few weeks Nick sat down for the first time and thought about the things that he really liked doing. He realized that his one constant interest since school was gardening – he had taken care of his parents' garden until he left home, and even though his current flat did not have a garden he still kept up a subscription to a gardening magazine and watched all the gardening programmes on television.

He took a course in organic gardening at his local adult college and placed some advertisements offering his services. That – and some good PR work by parents and friends – soon got him some regular clients. For the first time he had a job that he did not want to leave.

Scleranthus

Adrian plans to drop science subjects and concentrate on Modern Languages for the last two years of school. Then he does better than expected at Physics, and gets top marks.

Physics is a good bet for a career. Everyone knows there is a shortage of science graduates, and with a good science degree he will walk into a job after university. On the other hand, if he stays with languages he will probably have a better social life at university. There are always more women than men in language classes. And he will get to go to Latin America for a year if he takes the Spanish option.

He weighs it up, then weighs it up again. First one, then the other choice seems right. The more he thinks about it the more impossible it is to come to any kind of decision.

Remedy description

Scleranthus helps when we have a decision to take but can't make up our minds which way to go. Often the decision is a minor one, such as whether to see this film or that, or wear this or that dress, but important decisions can also leave us in a Scleranthus state – whether to go to university or start work, whether or not to get married. The key indication for Scleranthus is that we can identify positive options but can't take the next step and decide what to do.

The Scleranthus remedy helps to calm the indecisive mind so that we can take calm and rational decisions. By extension this remedy is often used when there are regular mood swings from one emotion to another (a lack of decisiveness at the emotional level, so to speak). Some people take it for motion sickness because they believe that emotional indecisiveness is the underlying cause of that particular problem.

Scleranthus is made from the tiny green flowers of *Scleranthus annuus*, which grows close to the ground on well-drained soil. It is prepared using the sun method.

Case discussion

Scleranthus people tend not to talk about the decisions they have to make. Adrian kept his indecision to himself and only confided in a friend when he was at his wit's end trying to decide. This is a clear indication away from Cerato, as is the fact that he did not know in his heart which way he wanted to go.

Sometimes people take Wild Oat whenever they have a potentially important decision to make. In cases like Adrian's, however, there are two reasons not to select Wild Oat. The first is that the question of his ultimate goal in life did not arise. The second is that he identified two desirable outcomes – better job prospects on the one hand, a better social life on the other. Wild Oat applies when there is no clear sense of what the options are, only a vague desire to do something worthwhile, while nothing seems particularly attractive. Being able to name desirable options but being unable to choose between them is a clear indication for Scleranthus.

EXERCISES
Walnut, Cerato, Scleranthus and Wild Oat

Suggest remedies for these people.

A One of Jan's friends from college has invited her to a party in London. Another has asked her to spend the weekend at his parent's empty flat in Edinburgh. She is not sure which one to go for.

B Should Paul ask Sally out for a date? He thinks he should, but he asks his friends' advice anyway.

C Aisha started nursing thinking that it would be a fulfilling career. Now she feels trapped and frustrated, but can't think of anything better to do.

D Jill lays the situation out for her friend's consideration. Should she take the fashion job in New York? This is what she really wants to do, and she has already drafted her letter of acceptance. Or should she remain in Chicago where her friends and family are, and stay on at university to do her PhD?

E Ed writes a school essay on his favourite book, *Peter Pan*. During the next lesson the English teacher mentions his choice and asks everyone to clap if they believe in fairies. From that moment on he is known as 'Tinkerbell', and he no longer enjoys reading his favourite story.

Clematis

Terry is 15 and wants to be a rock star. He dreams of forming a band – him on lead guitar and vocals, with a couple of girls on drums and bass – and has already thought of a name: Bad Samaritan. His is a single-sex school. There are three groups already formed and rehearsing, but he is only on the fringes of that crowd because he can't play an instrument. He has been saving for a guitar for a year, but he has nothing in the bank because he spends it all on CDs. Last week he got in trouble with the head teacher, who caught him drawing 'Bad Samaritan' on the desk in fancy writing when he should have been working on a maths problem.

Remedy description

Clematis people are dreamers and live wrapped up in their heads. They love to create fantasies of wonderful futures or alternative realities, but in a negative state they do not do anything to make their dreams come true. Their minds dwell on what may be and ignore what is, and as a result they may miss opportunities.

Many children go through a Clematis phase in which they ask their teachers to repeat things, fail to answer when their name is called, and fall asleep at the drop of a hat. If grown-up Clematis types are known for being artistic this is because they keep in touch with their dreams and fantasies throughout adult life. They can achieve great things if they can carry out their plans. The Clematis remedy can help them do this, because it doesn't prevent dreaming, but does bring dreams into focus. Castles planned in the air can go on to be built out of solid rock.

The remedy is made from *Clematis vitalba*, or old man's beard, the wild variety of this popular climbing plant. The flowers are prepared using the sun method.

Case discussion

This is a clear case for Clematis, although there is one additional remedy that Terry might think about taking, and that is Chestnut Bud. This is suggested by the way he repeatedly spends the money that should go for the guitar on more CDs.

Honeysuckle

Hannah is married now, and stays at home to look after her one-year-old baby boy. Ten years ago she was single and studying to be a veterinary nurse. She feels dissatisfied with her life as it is, and her husband, who works every waking hour, bores her. She loves the baby but spends a large part of her day thinking about things as they were before he was born, and before she got married.

Animals were always her great love. Looking back she can smell and touch them in her imagination. Things will never be as good again – she has no real future, only a past full of regret.

Remedy description

Honeysuckle and Clematis people are similar in that neither of them pay sufficient attention to the present. In another way, though, they are opposites. Where Clematis people daydream about the future, Honeysuckle people escape from the present by reliving the past. Sometimes they see the past as a golden age, never to be recovered, and at other times they brood over the things that went wrong.

The remedy helps us to focus more on the present and the future. We can learn from the past and be enriched by it without losing our ability to act and plan. It is made from the wild pink honeysuckle, *Lonicera caprifolium*, and prepared using the boiling method.

Case discussion

Walnut would apply if Hannah were trying to live in the present but being held back by her old life. But in fact she is using the past as a way of not dealing with the lack of a fulfilling relationship and career. This is clearly an indication for Honeysuckle.

EXERCISES
Clematis and Honeysuckle

Which person needs Clematis and which needs Honeysuckle? What does the other person need?

A Mary Beth's husband died several years ago. She looks forward to dying herself so that she can be with him again.

B School days for him were a golden time. Raj regrets losing touch with his old friends, and fantasizes that he is back in his final year arranging things differently.

C Claire moved out after her divorce and got a new job and a new life. She goes out on dates, but avoids all her favourite restaurants because she used to go to them with Gerald. She is no longer at ease in them.

Gorse and Larch

We have seen Gorse and Larch already. The first was introduced in Chapter 5, 'Depression and Hope', and the second in Chapter 4, 'Fear and Worry'.

Gorse is for people who give up because they feel pessimistic. The circumstances are hopeless so why bother trying? Larch is for people who are sure they personally will fail. Others could achieve success, but not them. Both of these states can prevent us from taking action, as can the next one we will look at: Wild Rose.

Wild Rose

When he left school Nathan got a well-paid job selling financial services over the phone. All through the 1980s he kept his job and did well at it. Then, in 1993, the investment house he worked for was swallowed by a multinational bank with a hard-nosed attitude to pay. Bonuses were cut. Many of Nathan's colleagues left to work for other companies. Nathan was one of the few who stayed.

With the loss of so many experienced salespeople it was only a matter of time before the new owners of the company decided to cut their losses. They withdrew from Nathan's market in all but name, leaving him and one other die-hard as a token presence. His colleague soon left. Still Nathan stayed – until the end came and the financial services side was closed down.

Nathan was unemployed for the first time in his life. He made a lot of noise about getting a new job, but took no real action. For a time he enjoyed living on his savings. But after six months or so he began to wonder where he was heading. Life had taken a wrong turning somewhere and he could not see where that had happened, nor find the impetus to do anything about it.

Remedy description

In a positive state, Wild Rose people are happy-go-lucky drifters. They like their pleasures and will not make sacrifices to achieve so-called higher ends. Indeed, the concept of 'achievement' is not important to them – they like to take life as it comes.

In a negative state the Wild Rose person moves too far into acceptance. He stops acting in the play and joins the audience. He falls into apathy and resignation. Instead of enjoying the drift of life he begins to feel that he is missing out.

The Wild Rose remedy is made from the beautiful pale pink flowers of the wild dog rose, *Rosa canina*. These are prepared using the boiling method. It helps bring life back into focus so that the Wild Rose person can see what is important to him and take action on that basis. It reawakens his zest for life. Instead of drifting he can be captain of his ship, and move forward with pleasure and a renewed sense of purpose.

Case discussion

Nathan showed the classic Wild Rose response to change when his company was taken over – he accepted and adapted and carried on as before. It was only much later that a long period of unemployment made him realize he needed to seize hold of his life and do something with it.

Wild Oat might have applied as well, but only if he had been ambitious to achieve something worthwhile and did not know what to aim at. We do not know that this was the case – we know that he wanted to stop drifting, but the simple act of getting another and similar job might have been enough to satisfy him.

EXERCISES

Wild Rose, Gorse and Larch

Select one remedy out of Wild Rose, Gorse and Larch for each
of these overweight people.

A It's no use me trying to diet – I just don't have the
willpower.

B I can't be bothered to go on a diet.

C I enjoy eating, so why bother dieting?

D I'm useless at dieting.

E Diets don't work.

F My weight problem is hormonal, so there's no point
dieting.

EXERCISES

Action and inaction

Jyoti has six more weeks of university left, and hasn't done
anything this month about getting a job. Supply more details of
her situation, actions or feelings, assuming that she needs these
remedies.

A Walnut.

B Olive.

C Hornbeam.

D Wild Oat.

E Scleranthus.

F Cerato.

G Clematis.

H Honeysuckle.

I Gorse.

J Larch.

K Wild Rose.

Recap

- Hornbeam provides the energy to overcome mental weariness. It helps when we feel disinclined to start a task despite being physically rested.
- Cerato helps when we distrust our decisions and seek out advice instead of following our own path.
- Scleranthus gives us the decisiveness needed to choose between options.
- Wild Oat helps us identify our goals and take a path that will bring us closer to them.
- Clematis anchors us in the present so that we can act rather than dream our lives away.
- Honeysuckle helps us live in the present and not in the past.
- Wild Rose gives us a sense of commitment to our lives, so that we can live to the full rather than drifting along.

Answers to exercises

Olive and Hornbeam

A Olive.

B Hornbeam.

C Hornbeam.

D Olive.

Walnut, Cerato, Scleranthus and Wild Oat

A Scleranthus.

B Cerato.

C Wild Oat.

D Cerato. (You could also argue for Walnut – she is making some attempts to move on but is being held back by old ties.)

E Walnut.

Clematis and Honeysuckle

> **A** Clematis.
> **B** Honeysuckle.
> **C** Walnut.

Wild Rose, Gorse and Larch

> **A** Larch.
> **B** Wild Rose.
> **C** Wild Rose.
> **D** Larch.
> **E** Gorse.
> **F** Gorse.

Action and inaction

Here are some suggested answers.

> **A** She started looking last month, but everyone else at university is partying.
> **B** She is too tired from studying to look for a job.
> **C** She cannot seem to work up the energy to get started on this – she'd sooner do more revision or go out.
> **D** She has no idea what direction she wants to take.
> **E** She cannot decide whether to apply for a research job or look for work in advertising.
> **F** She would like to work abroad, but she wants to find out what her brother and parents think before she does anything.
> **G** She is planning to become a best-selling novelist, though she hasn't yet written anything.
> **H** She is too busy sitting in the canteen with friends, reminiscing over the last four years.
> **I** There is no point trying for a job now, when there are so many university leavers in competition.
> **J** She is no good at interviews so there is no point applying.
> **K** Something will turn up.

10 GROUPS AND DIFFERENCES

Aims of this chapter

We have now looked at all 38 remedies. In this chapter we turn to Dr Bach's remedy categories, to see how we can use them to give us a further insight into the remedies. This will lead us to the question of 'subtle differences' – the fine lines between similar remedies – and to two techniques that we can use to make these differences come to life.

■ Dr Bach's seven groups.
■ Using the groups to highlight distinctions between remedies.
■ Situational groups.

Dr Bach's groups

Dr Bach presented his discoveries in a series of booklets. He published the first in 1933, when he had discovered 12 remedies, and called it *The Twelve Healers*. He found another four remedies that same year and published his revised findings as *The Twelve Healers and Four Helpers* (1933). As the title implies, he felt there was a difference in quality between the first 12 and the new four. The new remedies would be used when disease was well advanced and had affected the person's state of mind to the point where none of the 12 seemed to fit. A helper, he believed, would advance matters to the point where one of the 12 could be selected.

Dr Bach found a further three remedies, and kept the same healer/helper division in his next publication, *The Twelve Healers and Seven Helpers* (1934). He dropped it, however, following a year in which he discovered the 19 remedies that completed the system. When his final findings were presented as *The Twelve Healers and Other Remedies* (1936) there was no mention of helpers. All the remedies were of equal value and could be selected using the same simple process. He kept the title 'Twelve Healers' because his patients were so familiar with it, and although the original 12 were marked with an asterisk this was at the publisher's suggestion – they were not marked at all in the original typescript.

Instead of the broad healer/helper division Dr Bach categorized the remedies into seven groups. The headings he used were an echo of his early research into diseases of the intestine, when he had demonstrated a link between seven types of bacteria and seven broad categories of emotional state.

For those who have fear

- Rock Rose (terror)
- Mimulus (everyday fear)
- Cherry Plum (fear of losing control)
- Aspen (vague, mysterious fears)
- Red Chestnut (anxiety about the welfare of others)

For those who suffer uncertainty

- Cerato (seek advice)
- Scleranthus (cannot make decisions)
- Gentian (feel discouraged)
- Gorse (give up hope, despair)
- Hornbeam (tired at the thought of the task ahead)
- Wild Oat (ambitious but do not know which path to follow)

Not sufficient interest in present circumstances

- Clematis (dreamy, drowsy, living in the future)
- Honeysuckle (living in the past)
- Wild Rose (resigned to life, accepting what happens)
- Olive (exhausted by work or suffering)
- White Chestnut (repetitive thoughts)
- Mustard (gloom or despair with no apparent cause)

■ Chestnut Bud (failure to learn from experience)

Loneliness

■ Water Violet (independent, self-reliant, aloof)
■ Impatiens (quick and impatient)
■ Heather (talkative and self-obsessed)

Over-sensitive to influences and ideas

■ Agrimony (cheerful outside, troubled under the surface)
■ Centaury (find it hard to refuse favours)
■ Walnut (subject to outside influences)
■ Holly (hatred, envy, suspicion, spite)

For despondency or despair

■ Larch (lacking the confidence to try things)
■ Pine (guilt and self-blame)
■ Elm (overwhelmed by responsibility)
■ Sweet Chestnut (great anguish and suffering)
■ Star of Bethlehem (shock and loss)
■ Willow (bitterness, resentment, self-pity)
■ Oak (the limits of endurance and strength, steadiness to the end)
■ Crab Apple (feeling ugly or unclean, obsessive behaviour)

Over-care for welfare of others

■ Chicory (interfering, possessive)
■ Vervain (sense of injustice, over-enthusiasm)
■ Vine (ruthless, domineering)
■ Beech (lack of tolerance, critical)
■ Rock Water (makes rules and lives by them, sets an example to others)

In most cases we can see why Dr Bach chose to put remedies where he did. The 'Fear' category is straightforward, and 'Loneliness' does indeed contain remedies for three states that lead to loneliness

– Impatiens and Water Violet both begin by choosing solitude, while Heather has solitude thrust upon her. Mimulus, the type remedy for shyness and timidity, may also lead to loneliness, but is more directly related to fear and belongs in that category.

Turning to the 'Over-care' group, the spiritual strivings of Rock Water and Beech's lack of tolerance may not immediately suggest over-care for other people. But Rock Water people hope to show others the best way of living, and Beech people take the trouble to criticize and put to rights the many examples of bad living that they see around them. This is the sense in which they 'over-care' for others.

Other classifications present a deeper puzzle. Centaury, the remedy for people who enjoy taking care of others, is listed under 'Over-sensitivity' rather than 'Over-care'. Gentian and Gorse – the one for discouragement, the other for hopelessness and despair – don't come under 'Despondency or Despair' but under 'Uncertainty'. Indeed, if we go through the groups we find many remedies that seem to be in the wrong group.

We can't say for certain why Dr Bach grouped particular remedies in the place that he did because he left no notes. But if we look at some of the problem cases we may be able to make out the general principles that he applied.

Red Chestnut

Red Chestnut is in the 'Fear' category, because it is for a specific fear. But Red Chestnut concern is all for other people, so would it be better to class it under 'Over-care'?

If we look at the remedies in the 'Over-care' group we see that all of them care in a way that relates back to their own view of the world. Vine, Vervain, Chicory, Rock Water and Beech all feel they know what is best and try to influence other people to do things their way. Red Chestnut is different. The Red Chestnut person does not want to influence the way people live. She does not mind if you work well or badly, or what path in life you choose. She just wants to know you are safe, and suffers fear and anxiety at the thought that you might be at risk of harm. In this she is far more altruistic even than the Vervain, whose sense of justice bases itself on personal principles and a feeling of knowing what is best.

Dr Bach believed that controlling other people was a great mistake that could only harm the controller and the controlled. 'Any desire for control, or wish to shape the young life for personal motives, is a terrible form of greed,' he wrote. 'We must refuse to be under the slavery of greed, which compels in us the wish to possess others.' All the remedy states in the 'Over-care' group have their measure of greed and desire for control. The Red Chestnut form of care is different. It lacks ego – and the same lack of ego explains why Centaury does not appear in the 'Over-care' group either.

Gentian and Gorse

We can treat these two remedies together. Both come under 'Uncertainty' when we might expect to see them going under 'Despondency or Despair'.

The key here seems to be the question of faith and doubt. In a Gentian state we feel discouraged and doubt whether we can go further. With Gorse, we feel that all hope is gone. There may well be many possible ways forward, but we give up anyway. In both cases despondency and despair are not justified – we could overcome this state if we could get back our faith in progress and our sense of certainty.

Sweet Chestnut, a remedy that people often confuse with Gentian and Gorse, *does* appear under 'Despondency or Despair'. In classing Gentian and Gorse under 'Uncertainty', separately from Sweet Chestnut, Dr Bach demonstrates a difference of kind between discouragement and pessimism on the one side, and genuine anguish and despair on the other.

Hornbeam

Hornbeam is listed under 'Uncertainty', but would it be just as appropriate to put it with the other tiredness remedy Olive under the heading 'Insufficient Interest'? A clue to Dr Bach's thinking comes in his description of Hornbeam in *The Twelve Healers*:

> For those who *feel* that they have not sufficient strength, mentally or physically, to carry the burden of life placed upon them; the affairs of every day *seem* too much for them to accomplish, though *they generally succeed in fulfilling*

their task. For those who *believe* that some part, of mind or body, needs to be strengthened before they can easily fulfil their work.'

The emphasis here is mine, and shows that the Hornbeam state is literally all in the mind. If the Hornbeam person felt more certain of his strength the Hornbeam state would evaporate. In contrast, Olive people have suffered mentally and physically to the point of exhaustion. Taking Olive renews their ability to take interest in the world about them. Hornbeam people never really lost their interest in the world – as they discover when they gather enough self-belief to get started.

Mustard

Many users think of Mustard as one of the four classic depression remedies, the others being Gentian, Gorse and Sweet Chestnut. So why put it by itself in the 'Insufficient Interest' group rather than classing it under 'Despondency or Despair' or 'Uncertainty'?

The answer comes when we look at the relationship Gentian, Gorse and Sweet Chestnut have to their environment. Gentian and Gorse people pay too much attention to their circumstances, which is why they take it so much to heart when things go wrong. Sweet Chestnut people also respond fully to what is going on around them. Mustard people, however, feel unhappy when there is no external reason for that feeling. Things are going well and they should be happy. By putting Mustard in the 'Insufficient Interest' group, Dr Bach shows that Mustard helps us pay more attention to the real joys in our lives.

Conclusions

Dr Bach's division of the remedies into groups can seem confusing, but it was more than an editorial convenience. In *The Medical Discoveries of Edward Bach, Physician*, Nora Weeks tells of the 'infinite pains' that he took with the final version of *The Twelve Healers*, and everything we know of him and his commitment to simplicity tells us that he would not have included the groups without some clear purpose in mind.

It seems to me that Dr Bach's groups are essentially aids to selection. I do not mean by this that the selection process should start with identifying which group one should look in. That would be impractical and misleading. Rather, the groups come in towards the end of the selection process, and only where we can't decide which of two or three remedies to select. They offer us a further insight into the differences between remedies. We have seen how this works in the cases of remedies like Hornbeam and Olive, and we will see further examples in the next section.

Subtle differences

Bach practitioners refer to fine distinctions between remedies as 'subtle differences'. Subtle difference comes into play when two or more remedies might seem indicated for a particular feeling and we are having trouble telling them apart. For example, we might feel disinclined to apply for a different job even though we do not like the one we are in. We have resigned ourselves to staying where we are. Would Wild Rose or Gorse be the most appropriate choice?

Sometimes both will apply, but more often it is possible to narrow the choice down. This is worth doing, because if you take unnecessary remedies they prevent the ones you need from working as effectively. As a general rule it is a good idea to check whether one of two similar remedies can be ruled out before deciding to put both in the mix.

We can use two techniques to help us tease remedies apart. The first we have already looked at – using Dr Bach's groups. If we apply this to the Wild Rose/Gorse opposition we find that Wild Rose is for people who are not sufficiently interested in their circumstances while Gorse is for people who feel uncertain, and from there we can begin to put daylight between the remedies, knowing that the Wild Rose person's resignation is due to lack of interest, while the Gorse resignation bases itself on a lack of faith in the possibility of progress.

The second technique is to look at the indications for each remedy in turn and imagine yourself in your situation *as if* you were an archetypal case of first one then the other remedy. Then you weigh up the two caricatures you have drawn and decide which one is nearer to your actual emotional state. Reading the indications for **Wild Rose**, in that state **you would lack motivation to look for** another job and would accept without fuss the one you do not like ('they have surrendered to the struggle of life without complaint,' said Dr Bach). If someone showed you an advertisement for a good job you might apply, or might not, depending on which option was less trouble. In a pure Gorse state you would feel very pessimistic about the chances of getting another job. You would complain about your situation and your current job, and would appear more depressed. Your response to a job ad would be to explain why there was no chance of you getting the job, and if you were persuaded to apply you would do it without hope.

In both cases you would be resigned, but your feelings about being resigned would be different.

One or both of these techniques can help you find the differences between any paired remedy states. Nevertheless, there are some subtle difference questions that come up time and time again, and these reflect points where many people have difficulty. Some, such as Gorse/Sweet Chestnut and Olive/Hornbeam, we have covered already. Here we will look at a few more of these remedy pairs in order to point to the main differences.

Beech/Impatiens

We could describe both Impatiens and Beech as remedies for irritability. As Impatiens people delay irritates us, while as Beech people it is the way people are and the way they act that we can't cope with. This difference seems clear, but it can be hard to judge in practice, and Impatiens is often taken where Beech would be more appropriate and vice versa.

We have seen that Beech is in the 'Over-care' group, and this suggests Beech people want others to be like them. They take the time to criticize and put things right. Impatiens, on the other hand, is in the 'Loneliness' category. Impatiens people prefer to work alone because they believe they can get on faster that way.

Imagine that you are an archetypal Beech person working with someone else. She has done something silly – perhaps put some files back in the wrong place. Your reaction will be to tell her about it, possibly at some length. You may be openly critical of her, or you may keep your criticism just below the surface by explaining your own faultless filing system to her so that she feels two inches tall by the time you are through. As an archetypal Impatiens your overriding concern will be to get on with things. You are likely to fix the problem yourself to get it out of the way faster. You are unlikely to go into the why's and wherefores of what happened, as you do not mind over-much if she makes similar mistakes in the future, as long as you can get your current task finished and move on to the next one. You may even take on the rest of the filing yourself and give her some other job in another part of the building.

Beech/Impatiens/Vervain

Impatiens and Vervain people are quick minded and can get through a lot of work. Both tend to speak quickly and have forceful personalities. But Vervain is classed with Beech in the 'Over-care' group. Vervains will take time when things go wrong to explain to others a better way of working. They will not criticize on a personal level like Beech, and will try to be fair because they dislike injustice.

Vervain/Vine

Vine and Vervain people are both strong and determined. They feel they know what is right and want others to do things their way. The groups will not separate them, because both are in the same one. Instead we could use the same situation we looked at with Beech and Impatiens. How would Vervain and Vine react to the co-worker who makes a mistake with her filing?

Both would want to tell her the best way to do things, but it would be important to the Vervain person that she understand *why* it is the best way. For the Vine person it would be relatively unimportant what her colleague believed, as long as she did things properly. She would be inclined to issue instructions rather than teach and persuade, and would not want to discuss the rights and wrongs of the method.

Very out of balance Vine people become frankly dictatorial, and use the force of their personalities – or simple force – to get their own way. At their most extreme Vervain people can seem similar, in that their enthusiasm can turn into fanaticism. They no longer listen to other points of view, and also appear dictatorial as they lay down the law on what is right and what is wrong. At these extremes the problem of telling the two apart is harder, but the same test applies. The Vervain fanatic will want you to convert to her point of view. The Vine will insist that you do as she says, and you can keep your opinions as long as you do not act on them.

Vine/Chicory

Both are 'Over-care' remedies, and both can be overbearing and difficult to live with. Both feel they know what is best, and are happy to point this out to you, but there are differences in the way they do this, and they want different things from you.

An archetypal Vine tells people what to do in a direct and forceful way. He uses threats to get what he wants, or issues ultimatums, and he dominates family relationships by force. A Chicory is more subtle. The aim of his interference is to keep people dependent on him so that he can feel loved and needed. He is only trying to help, trying to be useful. If people turn down his offers of help he feels hurt and upset and resorts to emotional blackmail, something that the Vine rarely deigns to do.

Chicory/Heather

Both these remedies are for people who need to have others around them. Chicory is an 'Over-care' remedy while Heather comes under 'Loneliness' – and this points to an essential distinction. Both Chicory and Heather are self-regarding, but Chicory loves as well – she demands something back for her love, but it is love all the same. She lavishes care on people, and enjoys putting them in order and arranging their lives. Her concerns are for family, friends and colleagues, and she is less interested in strangers.

A neat distinction, which shows the relative lack of power and guile in the Heather person, is to think of Heather as the needy child, as opposed to the needy parent Chicory. An archetypal Heather person will seek out anyone's company in order to have an audience. She wants to talk about herself and her life, and she does not mind who she talks to, because her concern is with being listened to, not with who the listener is. In fact, she has little interest in other people and their doings.

Pine/Crab Apple/Rock Water

The potential confusion between these three remedies is that all can be very hard on themselves, and ready to condemn themselves. The differences lie in the underlying reasons for their self-condemnation.

Crab Apple people will condemn themselves for what they are. They feel that there is something rotten or unclean about them, and this is often related to a defect in their appearance that seems to them of overriding importance. Pine and Rock Water, on the other hand, condemn themselves for their acts and omissions. They do not feel they are bad people, but they do feel they have done bad things.

With Pine the cause is guilt. Sometimes they were responsible for an accident or for putting somebody else in a difficult position, but sometimes the responsibility was someone else's and the Pine person feels guilty for no good reason. When Rock Water people condemn their own actions, however, it isn't because they might have harmed others but because they have failed to live up to their own personal standards. Rock Water people want to be perfect, and condemn themselves when they fail to reach perfection. Pine people expect to be at fault, and blame themselves even when there is no reason to.

Sometimes there is confusion between Rock Water and Crab Apple for a rather different reason. This is because in their own way Crab Apple people also set themselves high targets. For example, the Crab Apple's obsession with cleanliness may lead him to be excessively house-proud. He may follow a strict cleaning routine, vacuuming and dusting from top to bottom three or four times a day. And the Rock Water's attention to detail may also result in a house where everything is in its place and visitors feel disinclined to sit on the beautifully plumped cushions or walk across the carefully brushed rugs.

The difference is in their sense of proportion. Rock Water nit-picks in the name of a system. He will be taking a wider view of things, and if he strips and varnishes the dog kennel every spring this is an act of self-discipline and demonstration. With an archetypal Crab Apple the big picture is lost in the pursuit of one small area of life.

The Crab Apple will go on cleaning and polishing while the walls fall down around him and his health suffers through lack of exercise. Rock Water pursues an ideal, but his Crab Apple neighbour concentrates on a tiny and unimportant part of life to the exclusion of any ideal.

Holly/Willow

Holly and Willow states are both categorized by negative feelings towards other people. The difference between them can be summed up in the phrase 'Holly blazes where Willow smoulders'. As this suggests, the Holly emotion is much stronger and burns quicker. The person in this state wants revenge and is bent on hurting someone. She looks outwards. Willow is turned inwards. The Willow person might still express negative feelings about others, but it will be resentment rather than revenge, and will tend to turn into self-pity.

EXERCISES

A It is two o'clock in the morning. A car alarm in the street has been going off every few minutes for over an hour and you are getting angry. How do you react if you need: 1) Cherry Plum; 2) Holly; 3) Willow?

B You are having trouble keeping your mind focused on your work. Describe your mental state assuming you need: 1) Clematis; 2) White Chestnut; 3) Honeysuckle; 4) Walnut; 5) Hornbeam; 6) Olive.

Recap

■ When writing up his final findings, Dr Bach split the 38 remedies into seven groups.

■ Experienced users of the remedies can use the groups to differentiate between apparently similar remedies.

■ Another way to decide which of two remedies is best for you is to imagine how you would expect to be feeling if you needed first one and then the other remedy.

Answers to exercises

A Your answers could be: 1) You are afraid you will lose control, go out into the street and attack the car or its owner; 2) You determine to get your own back, and next night when all is quiet you go outside and slash all four tyres; 3) You mutter and grumble about the alarm, and feel as if you have been singled out by fate, but you probably do not do anything about it.

B You might be: 1) Day-dreaming about your holiday next month; 2) Going over and over the argument you had this morning with your partner; 3) Thinking back to last week's summer holiday, and reliving every night out you had; 4) Affected by the atmosphere in the office, which is very subdued due to rumours about redundancy; 5) Lacking the mental energy to get started, and finding excuses to put off the task; 6) Exhausted after being kept up all night by your three-month-old child.

11 | WIDENING THE NET

Aims of this chapter

The remedies work to increase positive emotions. You can't make things worse, even if you get your selection wrong. The worse that can happen is nothing – and if the first mix doesn't work you can always try again. Knowing this should give you confidence to try out your selection skills on other people. This chapter will help you suggest remedies to your friends and family and encourage them to help themselves with the remedies.

- How to select for friends and relations.
- Basic listening skills.
- Ethical considerations when helping other people.
- Knowing when and how to get help.
- Special considerations when selecting remedies for children.
- Selecting for animals and plants.

Selecting for friends and relations

Friends and family provide plenty of opportunities for practising remedy selection, and because you know them already you will find it easier to suggest appropriate mixtures. You should start with the people you know even if you plan to go on to be a Bach practitioner, not least because you will feel less pressure to get results. Introducing the remedies to friends is as simple as remembering the bottle of Rescue Remedy in your pocket or handbag. But if you want to select a treatment bottle mix you should take a lead from professional practitioners and use some basic listening skills. Knowing how to listen means you can put your friend at ease, find out more about how she really feels and make a better choice of remedies.

First, make sure that you listen to your friend in a safe and private environment. Your home on a day when everyone else is out would be ideal, but a snatched conversation outside the school gates is less likely to give good results. Other people may put her off, so that she will not feel comfortable talking about her feelings.

Next, resist the temptation to ask deep, personal and probing questions. The remedies deal with emotions layer by layer, and you do not need to dig straight down to your friend's innermost hidden trauma. Stick to what is there on the surface. She will feel less threatened, and you will get there in the end. Also, try not to allow your own feelings about the situation to get in the way of what she wants to tell you. If she says she feels hard done-by, do not make her Willow state worse by agreeing with her that everyone has been rotten to her. Be empathetic, then, but be sparing with your sympathy. And try not to give advice – you are not there to sort out her problems. Your job is to give her space to off-load and open up.

If you ask questions, word them so that they can't be answered with a 'yes' or 'no'. 'How do you feel?', 'What did you do next?' and 'What does that mean to you?' are all open questions. They give people space to describe in their own words how they feel. On the other hand, questions such as 'Do you feel tired?' do not leave any room for discussion – all your friend can do is say 'yes, I do' or 'no, I don't'. Maybe tiredness is not an issue, but you are still getting her to think about it. Only use 'yes or no' type questions at the end of the conversation, when you want to close things down and check that you understood.

When we bottle up our emotions they quickly grow out of proportion, but talking problems through is therapeutic in itself. We think in words, so the attempt to put into words the way we feel will itself clarify what it is that makes us unhappy, and that is the first step to dealing with it. We may find our problems shrink as we discuss them, or we may gain new insights into why we feel the way we do. This means that by allowing your friend to let off steam you will be helping her even before she starts taking remedies – but if she finds talking about personal issues difficult you can take a more indirect approach. You might get her to talk about some everyday part of her life, such as her garden or job or social life, or listen patiently while she describes her physical symptoms. The subject of the conversation will not lead directly to a selection of remedies, but the way she talks will give you clues about her mental state. Remember too that listening to what people say is not the only way of reading what they mean. Tone of voice, speed or slowness in speech, silences, even breathing patterns can all tell you something. The same is true of body language. Slumped shoulders may indicate tiredness or depression. Leaning forward usually shows interest in what is going on, while leaning away may indicate anxiety or a need to keep distance.

Finally, a word about words. When we first learn the remedies most of us concentrate on the key words: Willow is resentment and bitterness, Vervain is enthusiasm and justice, Pine is guilt and Gorse is pessimism. When selecting for ourselves we can see below the words to the real emotions that we feel, but when we start helping other people the tendency is to stay at the level of key words. This can lead to bad decisions.

For example, your friend might say that she hates her boss. If you do not go further, and find out what she actually means by that, then you might assume an active, spiteful emotion and a desire to hurt, and pick Holly. But her real emotion might be very different. She might hate the way he does things, and need Beech to give her more tolerance, or hate to be around him because she is afraid of his temper, which would indicate Mimulus. Taking Holly will do no good, and your friend is likely to conclude that the remedies do not work and refuse to use them again.

To avoid this problem you need to get below the words your friend uses and find out what they really mean to her. Often the best way to do this is to ask an open question. In our example, asking her why she hates her boss will be enough to give you information on the real feeling obscured by the label 'hate'.

EXERCISES
Helping friends
Your friend has said that she feels depressed, and you ask her why. Imagine the different things she might say if she needs these remedies.

   A Honeysuckle.
   B Elm.
   C Gentian.
   D Willow.
   E Centaury.

Ethical use of Bach Flower Remedies

Laws governing the use of complementary medicine vary from country to country. In many parts of the world, including the UK, the USA and Australia, governments have adopted a liberal approach. As long as practitioners do not injure anyone or make wild claims about curing cancer the law tends to leave them alone. But other countries are regulated more strictly. In France only doctors and pharmacists can legally mix a treatment bottle for someone else, while in Italy simply writing 'take four drops four times a day' on a piece of paper is considered an act of prescription, and as such is illegal unless you are a doctor of medicine.

Of course, you are using the remedies with friends and family, and not charging money for your services. For these reasons you may not fall within the remit of local laws designed to control medical practice. Nevertheless there are certain ethical considerations that you need to bear in mind, even if your only 'client' is your husband, wife or child.

The most important is that you should not act without the knowledge of the person to whom you are giving remedies. I know of several people who have secretly dosed their partners' drinks and achieved good results. One can understand the motives for doing this, especially where a sceptical partner refuses help that he or she obviously needs, and of course the remedies can do no harm.

Nevertheless sneaking remedies into people is not acceptable, and not simply for legal reasons. One of the main aims of using the remedies is to increase self-knowledge. The remedies teach us about our moods and personalities, and help us to be more in control of our emotional and spiritual lives. Giving them on the sly is a denial of the other person's right to learn and be in control. In fact, if we feel drawn to do this it may say quite a lot about the remedies we need to take ourselves.

There are exceptions to the rule. We can hardly seek permission from a small baby before giving a remedy, and there may be times when a medical or other emergency makes the immediate offer of aid of paramount importance. Even in these cases, however, the exception should prove (and not become) the rule. As soon as your children are of an age to make decisions about remedies you should let them do so. Most children enjoy sharing in remedy selection well before their seventh birthday.

The next consideration relates to confidentiality and boundaries. If you help someone select remedies you risk stepping beyond the boundaries of your everyday relationship. It should be clear to you (and made clear to your 'client') that information revealed while selecting remedies is for the purpose of selecting remedies only. Not only will it not be revealed to any third person, but it should not affect your normal relationship with that person – though you will want to set limits to what you keep to yourself, as we will see in the next section.

Because the remedies are a self-help system you will want to encourage self-help in your friends and relations. Explain the remedies you are suggesting, and let people mix their own treatment bottles. This is the highest tradition of professional registered Bach practitioners, who seek to empower their clients so that they can use the remedies for themselves.

Finally, it is our responsibility always to explain that the remedies contain alcohol, in case the person we are helping has some religious or other objection to this. Again, we will look further at this question later on.

When and how to get help

If you intend to help other people with the remedies think now about what you will do if things get out of hand. You might learn more than you want to about someone's activities or attitudes, and it is as well to be prepared for this before it happens. Also, you need to be clear about where your own responsibilities begin and end. If someone tells you that he is involved in sexual abuse, or is stealing money from work, how will you deal with that?

There are few hard and fast rules here, and those there are vary from country to country. A good rule of thumb is to keep the things you hear confidential as long as doing this will not lead to someone else being harmed. If you can imagine justifying in court your decision to reveal something told to you in confidence, or – looked at the other way – you can imagine being censured for choosing not to talk, then you should probably talk to someone.

As to who you should talk to, again it depends very much on the situation. People with physical problems should see a qualified medical practitioner. Local social services might be a point of contact in some instances, or one of the many helpline services that specialize in abuse, drug addiction and so on.

On a more mundane – and more likely – level, you may find that you get so far helping someone with the remedies but then run out of ideas. Perhaps you are having trouble selecting the right remedy, or feel you have done so but without success. In these circumstances it is a good idea to have the phone number of your local professional Bach practitioner ready to hand, so that you can refer your friend on. You can find out who your nearest practitioner is by calling the Bach Centre. See the 'Useful Addresses' section at the end of the book for the number.

Special cases: children

Most children make easy patients, and talk freely about their problems. When communication problems do arise, such as with a very young child, try playing with him and looking at how he responds to things. Is he timid and shy (Mimulus) or bossy and determined to get his own way (Vine)? Does he fly into a temper when a toy fails to work properly first time round (Impatiens), or does he continue to try in a methodical way to get it to go (Oak), or simply give up (Gorse) or not seem bothered whether it works or not (Wild Rose)?

In many cases most of the information you have about a child's personality and emotions will come from a concerned adult. This will usually be one of the child's parents. If you are treating your own child it will be you. Whichever applies, give weight to the parent's views, but not too much. As parents we are accustomed to reading motives into the behaviour of children, and may forget that our readings are often inaccurate and not always impartial. You have to look at the things that happen to them from their point of view. What to you is a fun game that amuses your friends – such as holding out then snatching back a toy as a tease – might feel very different to the child, who is left frustrated and powerless. Children have to cope with punishment, verbal and physical. They struggle to communicate with adults who are wrapped up in their own affairs and reluctant to take the trouble to understand. They are left alone in the dark every night, perhaps with the half-understood echo of things seen or heard to haunt them. If they lose their temper they may be held so that they cannot struggle. They are made to share their favourite possessions with other children. Toddlers have a lot to cope with, and you will not help if you lump everything together and call it 'naughtiness'.

Usually children respond quickly to the remedies. This may be because their real feelings lie near to the surface. They have not learnt the art of concealment and self-defence that is second nature to adults. Where children do not seem to respond look at the family as a whole – and include yourself if it is your family. Emotional imbalances in a child may reflect and be rooted in a conflict between the parents, or between one or both parents and the children. The child will only be 'cured' when the tensions in the family have eased, which means in remedy terms producing individual treatment bottles for each member of the family.

The dosage for children is the same as for adults. Wherever possible make up a treatment bottle, using cider vinegar as a preservative rather than brandy, in order to minimize the amount of alcohol involved. For very young babies treatment bottle strength remedies can be added to a little cooled boiled water, or mixed with a formula feed. Nursing mothers can take the baby's remedies themselves and pass on the effects via their milk. Finally, external administration can be helpful with babies. A few drops gently applied to the fontanelle – the membranous area at the top of the baby's head – will transfer the effects well, and the action of stroking them in is soothing in itself.

EXERCISES
Selecting for children
What remedies might you consider in these cases?

A Monica is a quiet and shy little girl. She will be starting school next week and does not want to go.

B Graham is two, and his mother has just had a new baby girl. Graham has started having temper tantrums for no real reason, and this morning his mother caught him throwing toy cars into the baby's crib.

C Molly is ten and a dedicated ballet dancer. She had a very bad cold over Christmas and missed the chance to dance in the Christmas show. It is now mid-January but she still has a bad cough and is bringing up phlegm, and she feels very down in the dumps.

D David is ten days old. He screams himself to sleep but then wakes up after an hour and seems frantic and agitated. The doctor says there is nothing wrong. He had a long and difficult birth and his parents are so tired they don't know if they can cope with much more.

Special cases: animals

Many people use the remedies to help animals as well as people. The same principles apply – treat the emotional state and not the physical problem, and treat the emotions that are relevant now. There is an obvious difficulty, however, namely understanding how the animal feels about things. This is why many people only ever use Rescue Remedy. While this is effective up to a point, it will not address underlying problems.

With just a little effort we can go much further and attempt more accurate selections of remedies for the animals in our homes. Start by thinking about the way the animal behaves normally, and contrast that with the way it is at the moment. Try to see things through the animal's eyes. This involves a certain amount of anthropomorphism – pretending that your cat or dog is human – but it also means thinking the situation through without considering the effect on you. Many of us assume that cats spray the furniture and dogs destroy homes out of feelings of spite, or in order to get their own back, but from the animal's point of view 'spiteful' actions look very different. In most cases we humans have all the power and the animals respond to the situations we place them in with fear and anxiety. Your cat may see the new armchair as a disturbing alien object, and try to 'tame' it by spraying. Chewing up your shoes when you leave the house could be your dog's way of relieving its anxieties.

Knowing something about the species you are trying to help may help you select remedies for one of its members. Broadly speaking, some species of animals (including humans) are social and some are not. Some are eaten – they will tend to be more anxious and nervy – and others do the eating. Most run away when faced with danger, but some are more ready to fight than others, and some – including dogs – use fighting and the threat of fighting as a way of defining social position.

Look at the breed as well. When people selected which animals should breed with which they aimed at enhancing particular physical qualities – a fine nose for hunting, for example, or a special coat colour. They also selected for behaviour, to the point where each breed has a general personality of its own. Knowing the breed characteristics of dogs will tell you why a Chihuahua and a Yorkshire terrier will respond differently to the same cosy environment – the terrier is bred for aggression and a desire to hunt, and will explode with frustration if it can't express itself. I am not suggesting that all Yorkshire terriers have the same personality – that would be as simple-minded as saying that all white Europeans tend to be the same, or all Latins, or all ethnic Chinese – but just as Latins are more expressive than the English, so knowing the breed points us towards the mannerisms that different breeds will use to display the same inner emotion. A nervous Chihuahua will probably look frightened, while a nervous Yorkshire Terrier may threaten an attack.

Leaving Rescue Remedy aside, people give Holly, Mimulus and Walnut to animals more often than any other remedies. As a general rule, stop and think before you give Holly, because many people use it inappropriately and to no good effect. You might be treating a horse that bites or a snappy dog, but in both cases you should question whether hatred and spite are causing the behaviour. Even the dog that tries to dominate you or another member of its human pack does not do so out of spite. Vine would be more appropriate. Having said that, Holly would apply in cases where dominance accompanies an unreasonable and active suspicion of human motives, or in cases of genuine jealousy and spite between animals.

Most of the time you will use the remedies to help behavioural problems. Cats unsettled by a house move might get Walnut or Honeysuckle. Fear-biting dogs and nervous mounts could need Mimulus or Rock Rose. The remedies can also help where there is physical disease by addressing the emotional aspect of a problem while another treatment deals with the physical symptoms. Even if the problem seems purely emotional, however, it is a good idea to have your animal checked over by a vet – holistic or orthodox – in order to satisfy yourself that there is no organic reason for the change in behaviour.

Owners use a variety of methods to give remedies to animals, but each technique is designed to ensure that the minimum four drop treatment bottle dose is taken at least four times a day. The simplest is to drop remedies directly into the animal's water bowl. For small-to medium-sized animals add two drops of each selected remedy, or four of Rescue Remedy, to the water bowl. For bigger animals like horses and ponies add five drops of each individual remedy or ten drops of Rescue Remedy to every bucket of water. You do not need to worry about animals sharing bowls or buckets because the remedies will not do anything to animals that do not need them.

It may be that the animal hardly ever drinks – cats fed on moist foods get their water from their food – or perhaps you are trying to treat two or more animals with different remedies at the same time and they share water bowls. In the first case a simple solution would be to add the same number of drops to food. In the latter situation, though, you may need to make up a treatment bottle and give remedies that way.

You make up treatment bottles for animals in the same way that you do for people. The dosage is also the same – four drops four times a day – and it does not matter how big the animal is. You can give drops from the treatment bottle in a number of ways. Some people squirt them into the animal's mouth using the built-in glass pipette – though this could pose a risk if the animal bites through or swallows the glass. To avoid this possibility you may prefer to put the four drops onto a small biscuit or piece of carrot or any other treat that your animal will eat at once. Alternatively you could use the remedies to wet the nose or muzzle, where most animals will lick them off at once, or apply them to pulse points. In any event, the disadvantage of the treatment bottle approach is that you have to be on hand to give the remedies. This may not be a problem if you want to treat your caged hamster or fireside cat, but it can be a consideration if your nervous pony lives in a field five miles from your house.

Special cases: plants

The theory may be hard to understand – how can a form of life without a mind be said to have mental states? – but many people have used the remedies to help plants with good results. As with animals, most people stick to Rescue Remedy, on the theory that any problem can be described as a trauma, whether it is droopy leaves caused by over-watering or an attack by aphids. But again we can go further with a little imagination. Walnut has obvious uses during re-potting, planting out of seedlings and so on. Plants that do not thrive could be helped by Clematis, Wild Rose, Gentian or Gorse – experiment to find the right one – and the cleansing properties of Crab Apple are a good bet for any kind of pest or fungal attack.

The best and simplest way to use the remedies on plants is to water them in. This way the remedies stay in the soil while the plant absorbs them gradually along with the water. This means you can ensure a regular dose without having to water more than usual. For a houseplant, add two drops of single remedies (four of Rescue) and water as usual. For outdoor use the dose is about five drops of single remedies (ten of Rescue Remedy) per can of water. The same dose applies to trees. By watering all the ground shaded by the tree branches you will get remedies to the whole root system.

Another convenient method, good for freshening up dusty houseplants and waking up seedlings, is to use a water mister. Add two drops of single remedies (four of Rescue Remedy) to the mister and use in the normal way.

EXERCISES
Animals and plants
What would be likely remedies in these cases? Besides giving remedies, can you think of any other steps that might help?

A Henry was rescued when a cat breeder's was closed by the police. The owner had been mistreating his animals. Henry has been in his new home for three months, and is happy enough with his owner and other women. But he panics and runs away from men, however well-intentioned they are.

B Roger Rabbit lives alone in a wooden hutch in a back yard. He is rarely taken out of the hutch. If anyone tries to pick him up he bites.

C Gerty is a two-year-old mare. Her owner lives in a big house in the country, part of which is an old stable block. Here Gerty lives by herself when not being ridden, although she is turned out for an hour a day into a rough field at the back of the house. Every so often Gerty is taken to a show – but her owner is thinking of giving this up because Gerty gets over-excited and loses control when she sees other horses.

D An apple tree that was badly pruned last year and is no longer producing apples.

E A tomato plant that is producing split fruit.

Recap

■ The easiest way to start helping other people with the remedies is to offer them to your friends and family.

■ As well as listening to what people say, pay attention to the way they say it and to the things their body language tells you.

■ Ethical considerations when helping other people with the remedies include keeping what is said private, and only acting with the other person's full consent and knowledge.

■ Know your own limits with respect to what you can deal with and what you can keep confidential, and know how to get help when those limits are reached.

■ Children respond well to the remedies, and you can select remedies even for very young children using a mixture of play, observation and information from parents and other concerned adults.

■ When selecting for animals, consider the species and breed, and of course the individual characteristics of that animal.

■ The remedies can be used to help plants, although there might be a certain amount of trial and error involved.

Answers to exercises

Helping friends

Here are some suggestions.

A I keep thinking about Alan and wondering why things went wrong. I just can't get over it.

B I'm supposed to be organising the Christmas fair, but now mum's in hospital and needs cheering up, and I just don't know if I can cope any more.

C My first driving lesson didn't go well. I might as well cancel the next one.

D Everyone was invited to the party except me.

E They asked me to stay late to make tea for the meeting. I was hoping to start a language class this evening, but I'll have to cancel it.

Selecting for children

A Mimulus.

B Cherry Plum, Holly, Walnut.

C Crab Apple and Gentian or Gorse.

D For David: Impatiens and Star of Bethlehem. For his parents: Olive and Elm. The whole family might benefit from Walnut.

Animals and plants

A Star of Bethlehem and Mimulus. Henry could be helped by being gradually habituated to one male human over a period of days or weeks, if necessary with the help of an animal behaviourist.

B Mimulus or Rock Rose. Rabbits are social animals, and Roger would enjoy a hutch-mate and a richer environment. He should have daily gentle contact with his humans to give him a chance to get to know them.

C Cherry Plum and Vervain might help her keep her self-possession at the show, but the main thing Gerty needs is a friend. Horses pair-bond, so Gerty's owner might get another horse or pony to share the field with Gerty. At the moment she lives in solitary confinement – it's not surprising that she goes a little wild when she sees other horses.

D You could try Star of Bethlehem for the shock, and
Gorse as the tree seems to have given up.
E This is a trick question. The reason tomatoes produce
split fruit is because they haven't been watered
regularly. Perhaps the gardener needs some Clematis
or Chestnut Bud!

12 | TROUBLESHOOTING

Aims of this chapter

This chapter answers some of the most frequently asked questions about the remedies, including:

- ■ Why is the Rescue Remedy dose different?
- ■ What happens if you take too much of a remedy?
- ■ What do you do if you need all the remedies?
- ■ What happens if you choose the wrong remedies or cannot find a remedy that matches the way you feel?
- ■ Can remedies make you feel worse or cause reactions – and what do you do if this happens?
- ■ Can you mix remedies with other medicines?
- ■ Can you take remedies if you are pregnant?
- ■ How can you get help to select remedies?
- ■ When is it safe to stop taking them?
- ■ Can you make your own remedies?

How much should you take?

Here are the main ways to take remedies:

1 Put two drops into a 30 ml bottle of water and take four drops at least four times a day.
2 Put two drops into a glass of water and sip as required.
3 Put two drops straight on your tongue and repeat as required.

For Rescue Remedy, in all cases use four drops instead of two.

The first method gives you the minimum dose. Taking less than this will be much less effective, but taking more will not be more effective. The way to get over a crisis is to take more frequent doses.

You can take up to seven different remedies at one time. If you are using Rescue Remedy in a mix it counts as one remedy.

Why is it four drops of Rescue Remedy and two drops of everything else?

Rescue Remedy is a composite remedy and contains a smaller amount of each individual mother tincture than a single stock bottle. In strength it is something between a stock bottle and a treatment bottle. So in order to get the right amount of the remedy you double the dose.

Why is it two drops in treatment bottles and in a glass of water – surely the person taking the glass of water will get more remedy?

This is true, but the amount of remedy you take does not matter as long as you get the minimum dose – in other words the equivalent of four drops from a treatment bottle. When you take the remedies in a glass of water you are using more than you need to, but putting in two drops means you do not need to worry about how big the glass is or how much water is in it or how much of the water you have drunk. Even a single sip from a large glass should give you the minimum dose.

I can't get a 30 ml dropper bottle – could I use a different size for my treatment bottle?

In some countries the standard bottle size is different, or you may want to sterilize and re-use old stock bottles as miniature treatment bottles. The rule is to keep it simple. For any bottle size up to 30 mls add two drops of each individual remedy and (if you are using it) four drops of Rescue Remedy. So a 10 ml, 15 ml, 20 ml or 30 ml bottle should each contain two drops of single remedies and four of Rescue. If your bottle is bigger than 30 mls add one drop of single remedy (two of Rescue Remedy) for every 15 mls of volume or part thereof. So for example a 50 ml treatment bottle would contain four drops of single remedies and eight of Rescue Remedy.

If you follow these rules the dose from a treatment bottle will always be four drops, whatever the size of the bottle.

Is it important to add the drops before the water when making up a treatment bottle?

The standard instructions for making up a treatment bottle tell you to put in two drops of each remedy (four of Rescue Remedy) and then top up the bottle with non-fizzy mineral water. This is the way most people do it, but you can put the water in first if you want to. If you want to do this remember to leave enough room for the remedy drops – and for the dropper itself.

Some practitioners, who may be making up several different treatment bottles using the same bottle of water, prefer to add the drops to the water rather than the other way round. They do this in order to avoid the energy in the treatment bottle remedies 'leaking' back into the water bottle as the water is being poured. I have never known this to cause a problem, although I can't rule out the theoretical possibility.

I'm busy all day – could I take just one dose a day?

The recommended minimum dose is four drops from a treatment bottle, taken four times a day. This works out at 16 drops per day, so you could think of this as the minimum daily dose. This leads to the question: can I take my daily dose of remedies in two doses of eight drops, or one of 16?

If you find it impossible to take the daily minimum in four equal doses then two doses of eight drops or one dose of 16 drops will at least make sure that you take the daily dose. But a single dose a day is not as effective as four doses. Similarly, taking eight doses of two drops, or 16 of one drop, will not be as effective because each single dose is too weak.

In practice you can still space out the doses even if you are at work all day and have to leave the remedies at home. You might take four drops on first getting up, four drops an hour later on leaving for work, four drops on coming home and four drops before bed. The remedies will work better this way than they would if you took two doses of eight drops, or one of 16.

What if you take too much of a remedy?

You can't overdose on the remedies. Even if you drink a whole stock bottle in one go the remedies will not do you any harm. The brandy in the stock bottle might, however, which is why you should avoid giving undiluted stock remedies to children and pets and anyone else sensitive to alcohol.

What if you need all the remedies?

All of us need all the remedies at some time or another. This is because they treat common emotions that all of us can feel. That said, we do not feel all 38 basic states at the same time, and concentrating on what our dominant emotions are today is the key to cutting down the selection.

If you feel that you need to take a large number of remedies, start by leaving out any that relate to feelings that are now in the past. If you still have more than seven on your list, cut out the remedies that relate to passing moods and concentrate on those that relate to long-term or far-reaching moods, or describe you as a person. It should soon be possible to narrow down the choice. And you can always re-evaluate your selection at any time as new (or old, long-buried) emotions come to the fore.

Some people take another approach when they seem to need a large number of remedies. They take a catalyst remedy, in other words a single remedy taken by itself for a period of weeks in order to settle things down until the most-needed remedies can be identified. You can also use a catalyst if you have taken an apparently correct combination of remedies for many months without experiencing any improvement.

Dr Bach identified two catalysts, Wild Oat and Holly, the first for generally introverted and quiet people, and the second for intense, active extroverts. However, catalysts are very much remedies of last resort. They short-circuit the normal process of gradually peeling away layers of emotion, which means that you learn less from taking the remedies. Most people will never have to use them at all and good practitioners only recommend them once or twice in a year.

Is it always better to select as few remedies as possible?

In a sense it is better to select fewer remedies. You will hardly ever need to use more than six or seven at a time if you put a little thought into the selection process. Taking unnecessary remedies blurs the focus, and the ones that you do need will not work as well or as quickly as they might have done. That said, we should avoid taking the 'less is more' philosophy to extremes. If you genuinely need eight or even nine remedies, take them.

Why not mix all the remedies together and have a single mix for every problem?

Someone suggested this to Dr Bach, and he tried it out but found that it did not work. It seems that all the unnecessary remedies in the mix drown out the ones that are needed, so that nothing happens.

Are there any combinations of remedies that should never be used?

No. You could imagine circumstances where you might take two remedies that appear to be direct opposites (such as Vervain and Wild Rose, or Vine and Centaury). For example, you might have a Vine personality and be overbearing at work, but be in a relationship where you were playing out a Centaury role. You would need Centaury to help you set boundaries within the relationship and Vine to soften your harshness at work.

Do you always have to include your type remedy in a treatment bottle?

No. You only need to put into a treatment bottle the remedies you currently need. Nevertheless, the type remedy often is included because by definition it describes how you tend to react when things go wrong.

Does everyone have one single remedy that describes their type?

Usually there is one single remedy that fits better than all the others. But you might find that your basic personality is a combination of two or even three remedies.

What do you do if you can't identify your type remedy?

Just select remedies for your current emotional state. Eventually you will notice one or two remedies that seem to recur, and these may be your type remedies.

Does your type remedy change over time?

Type remedies describe your essential characteristics – who you are underneath all your changing moods. Because of this your true type is fixed. The one or two remedies that describe it will always be important to you, as they are the ones that help you stay in balance and express your positive attributes.

You might find that you start using the remedies and decide on a type remedy, only to discover something else underneath as the remedies strip away layers of emotions. This feels like a change, as if we are changing types, when in fact we are simply coming back to who we really are. For example, a shy, clever child sent to a boarding school might take on the role of class clown in order to cover his timidity and avoid being bullied. By the time he starts to use Bach Flower Remedies many years later he might appear the very incarnation of Agrimony. Only after that side of things has been dealt with will his real Mimulus character begin to come through. This is what we mean by peeling the onion, and it is often only at the end of this process that the real type will emerge.

What if you choose the wrong remedies?

If you take the wrong remedies they will do no harm, but they will stop the remedies you do need from working as effectively. Try to leave out any remedies you are not sure about. If it turns out you do need one of them you can always take it later on.

Taking all the wrong remedies will not make things better at all – but neither will it make them worse. The remedies are always and only positive in their effects, and can't bring about the negative mental states for which they are given.

How do the remedies work?

The short answer is that nobody really knows. Scientists have yet to identify the active quality in the remedies. People theorize about the presence of 'subtle energies' – but calling an energy 'subtle' is just a veiled way of saying that nobody has so far managed to isolate or measure it.

I have heard that the remedies work faster if you don't dilute them. Is this true?

No. There is no difference in potency or speed of effect between taking the four drops from a treatment bottle and taking neat stock remedy, although in the latter case the brandy in the stock bottle will taste stronger and this psychologically may give the impression that the essences are stronger.

I have heard that if you take a remedy for too long you will experience the negative state of that remedy. Is this true?

This is not true. The remedies are entirely positive and can't under any circumstances cause the negative state to appear.

What if the remedies make you feel worse?

In classical homeopathy this form of reaction is well known, and comes about because homeopathic medicine can cause the symptoms that it cures. This is the principle of 'like curing like'. Bach Flower Remedies can't cause negative states – indeed, this is one of the fundamental differences between the two systems. Nevertheless, sometimes people take them and subjectively feel worse before they start to feel better. This happens when the remedies bring to the surface emotions that have been wholly or partially repressed, and is part of the cleansing process.

The answer is to continue taking the remedies, adding any new ones that seem necessary, such as Gentian to overcome doubt about success, or Mimulus for anxiety that things will get worse. Rescue Remedy can also help you through a crisis.

What if you get a reaction to the remedies?

Occasionally mild rashes or similar temporary symptoms of the internal cleansing process may be seen, but these can be disregarded. Anything more severe has nothing to do with the remedies, and you should seek medical advice.

As for allergies, people allergic to brandy can have a problem, as brandy is used as a preservative. But the preparation methods used to make the remedies leave no physical trace of the plants themselves in the stock bottles. You can take Walnut if you are allergic to nuts, and none of the remedies will cause hay-fever, despite the heavy pollen content in the fresh flowers when they are picked.

What if you are already on medication?

You can use the remedies alongside any other form of medical treatment, whether orthodox or complementary. Again, the only exception comes because of the brandy used in the stock bottles. Some drugs react with tiny quantities of alcohol. If your doctor or pharmacist has told you to avoid alcohol take medical advice before using the remedies.

What if you cannot take alcohol?

If you are unable to take any alcohol for medical or health reasons then you may be able to use the remedies externally, by applying them to pulse points. Adding the diluted drops to a very hot drink will also help, as this will tend to evaporate the alcohol. However, once again you are advised to seek medical advice if in doubt.

If you have a religious objection to the use of alcohol then it may be possible to get special dispensation for medical use from your spiritual advisor, or once again apply the remedies externally.

Can you take the remedies in tea, coffee and so on?

You can put them in tea, coffee and fizzy drinks without any decrease in potency. You can even add them to food if you want to. In this they are very different from homeopathic remedies, which should be taken with a clean mouth, i.e. in isolation and not with meals or drinks.

Could you add drops to a bottle of mineral water – and if so, how many drops should you put in?

The amount of water or other liquid that the remedies are added to is not relevant as long as you get the equivalent of four drops from a treatment bottle each time you take a drink. You could add 16 drops from a treatment bottle to a litre bottle of water, and as long as you drank 250 mls at a time you would get the correct dose.

In practice you may prefer to take a few swallows from the bottle, or pour out a glass of water and drink from that a bit at a time. If there were only 16 treatment bottle drops in the bottle then each drink would contain less than four drops, and the remedies would be less effective. For this reason if you do want to mix remedies in a bottle of water you are better off putting in considerably more remedy – perhaps four drops of stock remedy singles, and eight of Rescue Remedy – so as to ensure that you get at least the minimum dose each time you take a drink.

Why do registered Bach practitioners insist so much on the 'four drops four times a day' formula, while others recommend any number of drops at different times and for different people?

Four drops four times a day is an effective dosage. Taking more drops at the same time is no more effective than four drops, so telling people to take larger doses wastes remedy. And telling people to take drops five or more times a day involves pure guesswork, for no practitioner can know how a client will feel day to day.

Registered practitioners try not to over-complicate the subject. Four drops four times a day is easy to remember and avoids the confusion that results when different people give out conflicting advice. Sometimes practitioners do feel that a client would benefit from taking the remedies more frequently, and will say something like 'take four drops four times a day, or more frequently if you want to'. This leaves the actual number of doses in the hands of the client, which is where it should be.

Do Bach Flower Remedies go off if they are stored near aromatherapy oils?

No. The brandy used to preserve the remedies may be affected and may taste a little strange, but the remedies will work just as well.

Are the remedies adversely affected by going through x-ray machines, bar code readers and so on?

No. Remedies go all over the world and scanning by x-ray machines and bar code readers goes on all the time. This has not caused any loss of potency.

What if you are pregnant?

You can take the remedies with perfect safety at every stage of pregnancy, and they will not harm you or your baby. Nevertheless if you have any concerns about this or any other aspect of your pregnancy you should always consult your midwife or doctor.

What if there is no remedy for the way you feel?

If you stay on the level of key words you will not find a single remedy for some complex emotions like sadness or disappointment or anger. If you feel disappointed, then, try to be more specific about what 'disappointment' means to you. Break it down into its components, or try to find its root cause, and select remedies for what you uncover. You might find resentment at being treated unfairly (Willow or Vervain), or discouragement (Gentian), or dissatisfaction with oneself (Crab Apple or Pine or Rock Water). The word 'disappointment' would not lead directly to your selecting Pine or Vervain, but by breaking it down these remedies become possible.

Are there more remedies to be found?

Dr Bach stopped looking for new remedies just over a year before he died, and was clear in his own mind that no further remedies would be needed and that the system was complete. Over the years his belief has gained empirical support since Bach practitioners have always been able to identify a mix of the 38 remedies for the emotional states that people present.

Nevertheless many people have borrowed Dr Bach's ideas and methods, and in particular the sun method of preparation, to produce remedies from thousands of different plants. Ranges of flower essences are now made all over the world, from Hawaii to Siberia. Often the producers market them as extensions to the system of 38. In my view, you can classify these new preparations under four possible headings:

1 they duplicate the action of remedies already in Dr Bach's system – in which case they are not needed within the system;

2 they treat 'secondary' emotions such as 'feeling blocked' and 'dislike of being touched' – in which case I would want to ask 'why do you feel blocked' and 'why do you dislike being touched' so as to isolate the elements that make up that state of mind, and so identify which of the 38 would apply;

3 they claim to treat specific physical problems, such as baldness or stomach pains – in this case, and leaving aside the question of whether or not they do what they say they do, they have no connection with Dr Bach's conception of medicine, which specifically works on the personality/emotional level;

4 they promise various improvements that will change you from who you are into someone better, faster, more sexually attractive, or more spiritually advanced – again this has no connection with Dr Bach's system, which is aimed at helping you be who you are so that you can learn from your life.

The world holds thousands of plants that help people, but the essences produced since Dr Bach's original discovery either do not improve the original system (adding more plants that do the same thing only makes it more complicated) or they have nothing to do with that system (they are based on a different philosophical/medical model). That is why there are still only 38 remedies in Dr Bach's system. They put us in touch with our higher, spiritual self so that we can develop at our own pace, whatever that pace may be, in perfect freedom from our ego's greed for immediate enlightenment.

Bach Flower Remedies were fine in the 1930s – but don't modern times call for modern remedies?

Times have changed and we have new things to be afraid of, new concerns, and new freedoms and responsibilities. People in Dr Bach's day did not fear AIDS and nuclear warfare, or worry about global warming or campaign against genetic engineering. But they did feel fear and worry and take part in campaigns. Only a genius or a fool could argue that our emotions now are somehow more complex than those of Shakespeare, Da Vinci or Dante.

Many of the best things about new age spirituality are restatements of old beliefs and practices. They bring us back to our roots and remind us of our relationship to the world, nature and God. We can see the remedies in that context – not as something outmoded but as something eternally renewed and timeless. They treat emotions rather than emotional triggers, and fear is the same now as it has always been, although the trigger for the fear may have changed.

What did Dr Bach die of, and why did he die so young?

In 1917 Dr Bach fell ill with cancer. Doctors gave him three months to live, but he lived on until 1936, and died then of exhaustion and not cancer. Because he was only 50 when he died people have sometimes asked why he could not cure himself. What this question ignores is that he did cure himself, every day, for 19 years – all the time it took for him to complete his work.

What if you need help to select the right remedies?

Even the most experienced flower remedy user sometimes needs a little help to see the way through a complex situation. And sometimes we see where everybody else is going wrong but can't see our own mistakes. For both reasons you may want to talk to someone who can take an honest and unbiased view and perhaps suggest the one key remedy that you have missed.

A Bach practitioner is someone who has trained to help other people use Bach Flower Remedies. They may work most of the time as counsellors or therapists or nurses, but when they work with the remedies they put these roles to one side and dedicate themselves to helping you see your own way through to the remedies you need. A typical consultation will be a one-to-one conversation, about an hour long, during which the practitioner will encourage you to talk about the way you feel.

To find a practitioner contact the Dr Edward Bach Centre in the UK (see the Useful Addresses at the end of this book). The Centre holds an international register of practitioners who work under a Code of Practice drawn up to ensure high standards of client care and practice.

When can you stop taking remedies?

You can stop taking the remedies as soon as you have dealt with your negative emotions. You do not need to go on taking remedies indefinitely, nor do you need to wean yourself off them gradually as you have to do with some conventional drugs.

Things happen in life to knock us off course, so the same – or different – negative emotions will surface at some time in the future. When this happens you can take the right remedies before the problem puts down roots, and this will make it easier to resolve.

Can you make your own remedies?

Many people enjoy the experience of making their own flower remedies, and the process itself is quite simple. But you do need to bear a few things in mind.

First, it is essential to use the right plant. Other plants – even very close relations – will not give the required effect. Indeed, with Impatiens even the colour of the flower is a consideration, as only the very pale mauve flowers have the right healing quality.

Second, treat wild flowers with respect. In many parts of the world they enjoy some form of legal protection, and if you pick flowers without being sure what you are doing you may be destroying rare plants. It is almost certainly illegal, wherever you live, to pick flowers without the permission of the landowner.

Third, you need to use the right method of preparation for the plant that you want to prepare. Twenty of the remedies must be prepared using the sun method and the remainder must be prepared using the boiling method.

Sun method

Agrimony	Oak
Centaury	Olive
Cerato	Rock Rose
Chicory	Rock Water
Clematis	Scleranthus
Gentian	Vervain
Gorse	Vine
Heather	Water Violet
Impatiens	White Chestnut
Mimulus	Wild Oat

Boiling method

Aspen	Larch
Beech	Mustard
Cherry Plum	Pine
Chestnut Bud	Red Chestnut
Crab Apple	Star of Bethlehem
Elm	Sweet Chestnut
Holly	Walnut
Honeysuckle	Wild Rose
Hornbeam	Willow

As for the methods of preparation, these were described by Dr Bach in the 1936 edition of *The Twelve Healers*.

The sun method

A thin glass bowl is taken and almost filled with the purest water obtainable, if possible from a spring nearby.

The blooms of the plant are picked and immediately floated on the surface of the water, so as to cover it, and then left in the bright sunshine for three or four hours, or less time if the blooms begin to show signs of fading. The blossoms are then carefully lifted out and the water poured into bottles so as to half fill them. The bottles are then filled up with brandy to preserve the remedy.

Figure 12.1   The sun method

The boiling method

The specimens . . . were boiled for half an hour in clean pure water.

The fluid strained off, poured into bottles until half filled, and then, when cold, brandy added as before to fill up and preserve.

Chestnut Bud. For this remedy the buds are gathered from the White Chestnut tree, just before bursting into leaf.

In others the blossom should be used together with small pieces of stem or stalk and, when present, young fresh leaves.

Figure 12.2 The boiling method

The resulting mother tinctures can be further diluted before use, as described in Chapter 1.

Making a remedy can be an uplifting and peaceful experience, and a chance to get closer to the essential simplicity of the remedies and of course to nature itself. If this side of things interests you then your first step should be to get a copy of *Bach Flower Remedies: Illustrations and Preparations* by Nora Weeks and Victor Bullen. This contains full descriptions of the plants used and instructions for preparing them.

GLOSSARY AND REPERTORY

Glossary

The glossary gives a brief definition of specialist terms such as *treatment bottle* and *higher self* and lists all the remedies with their basic indications. You will find full indications for the remedies in the main text.

Agrimony   Remedy for people who hide their fears and worries by laughing at them.

Aspen   Remedy for people who are frightened or anxious but cannot give a reason for their fear.

Beech   Remedy for people who criticize other people's lives and actions, and lack tolerance.

Boiling Method   The method used to make 18 of the 38 remedies. Flowering twigs or stalks are boiled in water for half an hour then left to cool. The energized water is then mixed 50:50 with brandy to make the *mother tincture*.

Catalyst   A remedy given by itself in order to clarify what other remedies are needed. Dr Bach identified two catalysts, Wild Oat and Holly.

Centaury   Remedy for people who have trouble refusing the demands of others.

Cerato   Remedy for people who do not trust their own judgement, and as a result ask other people for advice.

Cherry Plum   Remedy for loss of control and the fear of losing control.

Chestnut Bud   Remedy for people who repeat their mistakes and are slow to learn from experience.

Chicory Remedy for people who insist on helping and controlling the people they love.

Clematis Remedy to ground people who live in dreams rather than the present.

Crab Apple Remedy for people who dislike themselves and the way they look; the cleansing remedy.

Elm Remedy for people who take on a lot of responsibility but sometimes doubt their ability to cope.

Gentian Remedy for people who feel despondent after something has gone wrong.

Gorse Remedy for people who give up hope after something has gone wrong even when the way ahead is clear.

Heather Remedy for people who talk to excess about their day-to-day lives.

Higher self In Dr Bach's philosophy, the immortal part of a human being, which incarnates on earth through the personality.

Holly Remedy for intense negative feelings towards other people, such as hatred, envy and spite.

Honeysuckle Remedy for thoughts that circle around the past, such as homesickness, regrets, nostalgia.

Hornbeam Remedy for mental tiredness that comes at the thought of starting work.

Impatiens Remedy for impatient people who live life in a rush.

Larch Remedy for people who think of themselves as failures, and lack the confidence to try.

Mimulus Remedy for everyday fears and for shy, timid people.

Minimum dose Four drops from a *treatment bottle*.

Mood remedy A word used to describe any remedy when it is used to treat a passing mood.

Mother tincture A 50:50 mixture of water that has been energized using either the *sun method* or *boiling method*, and brandy.

Mustard Remedy for sad, gloomy states for which there is no apparent reason in the person's life.

Oak   Remedy for steady, strong people who struggle on through every difficulty.

Olive   Remedy for tiredness that comes after some physical, mental or emotional effort.

Personality   In Dr Bach's philosophy, the incarnation on earth of the *higher self*. Can be thought of as the ego, or the mind.

Pine   Remedy for people who feel guilty.

Red Chestnut   Remedy for people who are overly anxious about the welfare of the people they love.

Rescue Cream   A mix of *Rescue Remedy* and *Crab Apple* in a homeopathically prepared cream, designed for external application.

Rescue Remedy   A formulation of five remedies – *Star of Bethlehem, Rock Rose, Impatiens, Clematis* and *Cherry Plum*, which is used as a first-aid remedy to overcome crises and stressful situations.

Rock Rose   Remedy for panic and extreme terror.

Rock Water   Remedy for people who live by strict rules, and drive themselves toward martyrdom.

Scleranthus   Remedy for people who cannot make up their minds.

Star of Bethlehem   Remedy for shock.

Stock remedy   A dilution of two-thirds of a drop of *mother tincture* to 10 mls of brandy. This is the strength remedy usually found in shops.

Sun method   The method used to make 20 of the 38 remedies. Flowers are floated on water in the sun for three hours. The energized water is then mixed 50:50 with brandy to make the *mother tincture*.

Sweet Chestnut   Remedy for extreme anguish and despair, when every way forward is blocked.

Treatment bottle   A dilution of two drops of a *stock remedy* (or of several stock remedies) in 30 mls of water. The dosage from a treatment bottle is four drops four times a day.

Type remedy   A remedy that defines a basic character type.

Vervain   Remedy for people who are very enthusiastic about what they do, and for those made especially angry by injustice.

Vine   Remedy for strong leaders who may use force and bullying to get their own way.

Walnut   Remedy for people who are being held back by outside influences; for help at times of change.

Water Violet   Remedy for self-sufficient, aloof people who like solitude but find that this turns to loneliness.

White Chestnut   Remedy for repetitive worrying thoughts.

Wild Oat   Remedy for people who feel dissatisfied at the way life is going but do not know what direction to take.

Wild Rose   Remedy for people who accept what life brings and do not take an active role.

Willow   Remedy for people who feel sorry for themselves, or resentful and bitter, and blame other people for their situation.

Repertory

The repertory is organized under headings and subheadings. First look for the word that best describes the way you feel or behave, then find the subheading that seems to relate best to you. This leads you to a particular named remedy. For example, if you are anxious about your husband's health look for the main heading *Anxiety*. Under the subheading *about someone's welfare* you will find the suggested remedy is Red Chestnut.

Everyone uses words differently, and you may have to think of other words for your state of mind before hitting on the key word used here. The remedy (or remedies) that you arrive at is not a sure and certain choice, and others may apply in particular circumstances. Before taking a remedy you should check its full indications in the main text.

Absent-mindedness
- ... through daydreaming – Clematis
- ... through nostalgia – Honeysuckle

■ . . . because of worrying thoughts – White Chestnut, Mimulus

Accidents

■ . . . for immediate help – Rescue Remedy

■ . . . for terror – Rock Rose

Aggression

■ . . . because of intolerance or to express criticism – Beech

■ . . . uncontrolled – Cherry Plum

■ . . . taking revenge, or through spite or hatred – Holly

■ . . . irritability at delay – Impatiens

■ . . . in pursuit of a cause or against injustice – Vervain

■ . . . in order to get your own way – Vine

Ambitions

■ . . . stifled due to other people's demands – Centaury

■ . . . plans never carried out – Clematis

■ . . . lack of confidence to try things – Larch

■ . . . pursued at the expense of pleasure – Rock Water

■ . . . vague ambitions with no sense of direction – Wild Oat

■ . . . lack of ambition – Wild Rose

Anger see *Aggression*

Anxiety

■ . . . for no good reason – Aspen

■ . . . due to a definite cause – Mimulus

■ . . . about someone's welfare – Red Chestnut

■ . . . great fear and terror – Rock Rose

Arrogance

■ . . . expressed through criticism of others – Beech

■ . . . controlling the lives of loved ones – Chicory

■ . . . thinks others are too slow – Impatiens

■ . . . spiritual pride, making a show of perfection – Rock Water

■ . . . fanaticism for a point of view – Vervain
■ . . . refusal to listen to advice, domineering – Vine
■ . . . private and aloof, appears proud – Water Violet

Assertiveness (lack of)

■ . . . through lack of faith in one's judgement – Cerato
■ . . . because of dreaminess, other-worldliness – Clematis
■ . . . through lack of confidence – Larch
■ . . . through shyness, timidity – Mimulus
■ . . . through indecision – Scleranthus
■ . . . through apathy – Wild Rose

Attention-seeking

■ . . . among family and friends, to get affection – Chicory
■ . . . talkative and clingy, even with strangers – Heather
■ . . . making a show of perfection – Rock Water
■ . . . grumbling and complaining – Willow

Bitterness

■ . . . over other people's ingratitude – Chicory
■ . . . about past events – Honeysuckle
■ . . . over unfair treatment – Willow

Calm (lack of)

■ . . . inner torment masked by a sense of humour – Agrimony
■ . . . vague fears, free-floating anxiety – Aspen
■ . . . loss of self-control – Cherry Plum
■ . . . in a rush, agitated – Impatiens
■ . . . due to everyday anxieties – Mimulus
■ . . . tortured by guilt – Pine
■ . . . through concerns over other people's welfare – Red Chestnut
■ . . . great terror – Rock Rose
■ . . . extreme mental anguish – Sweet Chestnut
■ . . . over-enthusiasm – Vervain
■ . . . because of change or outside influences – Walnut

■ . . . chattering, repetitive thoughts – White Chestnut

Clumsiness

■ . . . through failure to learn something – Chestnut Bud

■ . . . because mind is elsewhere – Clematis

■ . . . through trying to go too fast – Impatiens

Conceit see *Arrogance*

Concentration (lack of)

■ . . . failure to learn from experience – Chestnut Bud

■ . . . daydreaming, mind wandering – Clematis

■ . . . due to talking too much – Heather

■ . . . due to reliving past events – Honeysuckle

■ . . . putting things off, delaying the start of work – Hornbeam

■ . . . through going too fast – Impatiens

■ . . . due to outside factors – Walnut

■ . . . due to worrying thoughts – White Chestnut

■ . . . due to lack of interest – Wild Rose

Confidence (lack of)

■ . . . due to vague fears – Aspen

■ . . . in one's decisions – Cerato

■ . . . in one's appearance – Crab Apple

■ . . . in one's ability to cope with many responsibilities – Elm

■ . . . in one's ability to make a success of something – Larch

■ . . . due to anxiety in social situations etc. – Mimulus

■ . . . due to always being at fault – Pine

Criticism

■ . . . of other people, other lifestyles – Beech

■ . . . of one's own ability to take decisions – Cerato

■ . . . of family and friends, for lack of gratitude – Chicory

■ . . . of one's own appearance or nature – Crab Apple

■ . . . of other people's slowness – Impatiens

■ . . . of one's own inability to do something – Larch

■ . . . of oneself because of a wrong action – Pine

■ . . . of oneself for being weak, not keeping to a plan – Rock Water

■ . . . of injustice and unfairness – Vervain

■ . . . of other people for their luck and success – Willow

Cruelty

■ . . . through criticism – Beech

■ . . . spiteful and vindictive – Holly

■ . . . in the name of a cause – Vervain

■ . . . to enforce one's will – Vine

Depression

■ . . . masked by humour and good living – Agrimony

■ . . . caused by exaggerated feelings of rejection – Chicory

■ . . . due to feeling unclean or unlovable – Crab Apple

■ . . . due to too much responsibility – Elm

■ . . . mild, due to a setback – Gentian

■ . . . when something feels hopeless – Gorse

■ . . . associated with regrets over past events – Honeysuckle

■ . . . with no apparent cause – Mustard

■ . . . due to a loss or a shock – Star of Bethlehem

■ . . . extreme, when all hope is gone – Sweet Chestnut

■ . . . grumbling, negative and self-pitying – Willow

Despair see *Depression*

Direction see *Ambitions*

Disappointment

■ . . . at someone else's lack of gratitude – Chicory

■ . . . following a set-back – Gentian

■ . . . with the present compared with the past – Honeysuckle

■ . . . with one's own actions – Pine, Rock Water

■ . . . with one's lot in life compared with others – Willow

Disgust

- ... at other people's lifestyles – Beech
- ... or dirt; and at one's own nature or appearance – Crab Apple
- ... for one's actions – Pine
- ... for one's lack of will-power – Rock Water, Centaury

Dissatisfaction see *Disappointment*

Domineering

- ... critical and intolerant – Beech
- ... within the family or group – Chicory
- ... due to fanaticism – Vervain
- ... to get one's own way – Vine

Doubt

- ... about one's ability to make right decisions – Cerato
- ... about one's self-control – Cherry Plum
- ... about whether one is loved enough – Chicory
- ... about one's appearance or self-worth – Crab Apple
- ... over one's ability to cope with responsibilities – Elm
- ... over one's ability to overcome a set-back – Gentian
- ... about the possibility of finding a solution – Gorse
- ... suspicion of someone's actions or motives – Holly
- ... over one's strength to begin a task – Hornbeam
- ... about one's ability to succeed – Larch
- ... about someone else's safety – Red Chestnut
- ... about what option to choose – Scleranthus
- ... caused by other people's views – Walnut
- ... over one's path in life – Wild Oat

Egoism

- ... criticizing others – Beech

■ . . . wanting loved ones to live under one's control – Chicory

■ . . . does not listen to others – Heather

■ . . . trying to perfect the self – Rock Water

■ . . . forcing others to obey – Vine

■ . . . appearing proud, stand-offish – Water Violet

Envy see *Jealousy*

Exhaustion

■ . . . due to doing other people's work and not one's own – Centaury

■ . . . due to having too much responsibility – Elm, Oak

■ . . . at the mere thought of starting a task – Hornbeam

■ . . . due to long, sustained effort against all odds – Oak

■ . . . after effort – Olive

■ . . . due to having pushed oneself too hard – Rock Water, Vervain

■ . . . accompanied by apathy – Wild Rose

Exploitation

■ . . . by others – Centaury

■ . . . of friends and family – Chicory

■ . . . of other people – Vine

■ . . . feeling exploited – Willow

Failure

■ . . . to deal with worries effectively – Agrimony

■ . . . to follow one's own path in life – Centaury, Walnut

■ . . . to trust one's own judgement – Cerato

■ . . . to learn from experience – Chestnut Bud

■ . . . to act on one's dreams – Clematis

■ . . . feared, due to number of responsibilities – Elm

■ . . . to get started – Hornbeam

■ . . . expected, so that there is no point trying – Larch

■ . . . blamed on oneself – Pine

■ . . . to meet targets leads to self-condemnation –
Rock Water

■ . . . to decide between options – Scleranthus

■ . . . due to outside influences – Walnut

■ . . . to find one's path in life – Wild Oat

■ . . . blamed on other people – Willow

Faith see *Doubt*

Fanaticism

■ . . . with criticism of others – Beech, Vervain

■ . . . about cleanliness and unimportant details – Crab
Apple

■ . . . about self improvement – Rock Water

■ . . . with a need to gain converts – Vervain

Fear see *Anxiety*

Forgetfulness

■ . . . of one's own needs – Centaury

■ . . . of lessons learned in the past – Chestnut Bud

■ . . . with daydreaming – Clematis

■ . . . of the present with remembrance of the past –
Honeysuckle

■ . . . due to going too fast – Impatiens

■ . . . of self because of fears for someone else – Red
Chestnut

■ . . . due to a chattering mind – White Chestnut

■ . . . through lack of effort – Wild Rose

Frustration

■ . . . at other people's stupidity – Beech

■ . . . due to doing things for other people – Centaury

■ . . . due to lack of patience – Impatiens

■ . . . due to lack of outlet for one's enthusiasm –
Vervain

■ . . . due to outside influences – Walnut

■ . . . due to lack of a goal in life – Wild Oat

Guilt

■ . . . with or without a cause – Pine

Hatred

■ . . . of oneself – Crab Apple

■ . . . of someone else – Holly

Helplessness

■ . . . covered up with a smiling face – Agrimony

■ . . . through inability to stand up for oneself – Centaury

■ . . . to control one's violent impulses – Cherry Plum

■ . . . to control compulsive behaviour – Crab Apple

■ . . . at the number of responsibilities one has – Elm

■ . . . due to loss of hope – Gorse

■ . . . due to lack of confidence – Larch

■ . . . at having to make a decision – Scleranthus

■ . . . to control one's thoughts – White Chestnut

Homesickness

■ . . . due to living in the past – Honeysuckle

■ . . . mild, despite best efforts at living in the present – Walnut

Impulsiveness

■ . . . leads to repeating the same mistakes – Chestnut Bud

■ . . . due to lack of patience – Impatiens

■ . . . due to over-enthusiasm – Vervain

Inconsistency

■ . . . due to being dominated by someone else – Centaury

■ . . . due to seeking out conflicting advice – Cerato

■ . . . due to loss of rationality – Cherry Plum

■ . . . due to inattention to what is going on – Clematis

■ . . . due to lack of confidence – Larch

■ . . . due to sudden, unexplained depression – Mustard

■ . . . due to indecision – Scleranthus

■ . . . due to flights of enthusiasm – Vervain

■ . . . due to outside influences or ideas – Walnut

■ . . . due to lack of a clear direction – Wild Oat

Indifference

- ■ ... to one's own needs – Centaury, Red Chestnut
- ■ ... to the lessons of experience – Chestnut Bud
- ■ ... to other people's need for freedom – Chicory
- ■ ... to what is going on in the present – Clematis, Honeysuckle
- ■ ... to the thoughts and experiences of other people – Heather
- ■ ... to the needs of others – Vine
- ■ ... to life – Wild Rose, Clematis

Inferiority

- ■ ... shown by willingness to be enslaved – Centaury
- ■ ... when it comes to taking decisions – Cerato
- ■ ... in terms of personal appearance – Crab Apple
- ■ ... because of a lack of confidence – Larch
- ■ ... because of anxiety or shyness – Mimulus
- ■ ... because of guilt over one's actions – Pine

Inhibited

- ■ ... by the forcefulness of other people – Centaury
- ■ ... through feeling unattractive or ashamed of oneself – Crab Apple
- ■ ... by one's lack of confidence – Larch
- ■ ... because of shyness – Mimulus
- ■ ... because of guilt – Pine
- ■ ... through self-denial and repression – Rock Water
- ■ ... by one's surroundings or the opinions of others – Walnut

Irritability

- ■ ... because of a lack of tolerance – Beech
- ■ ... with loss of control – Cherry Plum
- ■ ... at any delay – Impatiens
- ■ ... with oneself for any failure – Rock Water
- ■ ... used to get one's own way – Vine
- ■ ... coupled with self-pity – Willow

Isolation see *Solitude*

Jealousy

■ . . . through a desire to possess loved ones – Chicory
■ . . . with suspicion or spite – Holly
■ . . . of other people's happiness – Willow

Learning

■ . . . inability to learn – Chestnut Bud
■ . . . made difficult by lack of attention – Clematis

Loneliness see *Solitude*

Loss

■ . . . of will-power – Centaury
■ . . . of energy – Olive
■ . . . with grief, or with a shock – Star of Bethlehem
■ . . . of all hope – Sweet Chestnut

Negativity see *Pessimism*

Nervousness see *Anxiety*

Obstinacy

■ . . . in seeing only one way to do things – Beech
■ . . . in repeating mistakes – Chestnut Bud
■ . . . in carrying on at the same pace – Oak
■ . . . in pursuing a path regardless of cost – Rock Water
■ . . . in trying to persuade others – Vervain
■ . . . with dominance and inflexibility – Vine

Over-sensitive see *Sensitivity*

Overwork

■ . . . due to not saying 'no' to a request – Centaury
■ . . . caused by the weight of responsibility – Elm
■ . . . due to trying to do things too quickly – Impatiens
■ . . . with long hours of steady effort – Oak
■ . . . leading to exhaustion – Olive
■ . . . due to setting oneself unreasonable targets – Rock Water
■ . . . due to over-enthusiasm – Vervain

Perfectionism

■ . . . nit-picking, with criticism of others – Beech

■ . . . intrusive, with attempts to direct loved ones – Chicory

■ . . . in small things, while the big picture is not seen – Crab Apple

■ . . . regarding self, by living up to a set of standards – Rock Water

■ . . . coupled with enthusiasm – Vervain

Pessimism

■ . . . with foreboding that something bad will happen – Aspen

■ . . . mild, following a set-back – Gentian

■ . . . with the decision to abandon hope – Gorse

■ . . . over the future compared with the past – Honeysuckle

■ . . . over one's strength to start a task – Hornbeam

■ . . . over one's ability to do something – Larch

■ . . . for no reason – Mustard

■ . . . over one's bad luck – Willow

Possessiveness

■ . . . for the affection of friends and family – Chicory

■ . . . for people's time and attention – Heather

■ . . . with jealousy and suspicion – Holly

Pride see *Arrogance*

Relaxation (lack of)

■ . . . worries surface when alone – Agrimony

■ . . . vague fears and anxiety – Aspen

■ . . . due to agitation, going too fast – Impatiens

■ . . . due to denying oneself time to relax – Rock Water

■ . . . due to over-enthusiasm, being a workaholic – Vervain

Resignation

■ . . . due to loss of hope – Gorse

■ . . . due to feeling incapable of making successful changes – Larch

■ . . . due to apathy and lack of interest – Wild Rose

Resilience

■ . . . appearing brave and cheerful but suffering underneath – Agrimony

■ . . . strong, determined and steady until health fails – Oak

Restlessness

■ . . . at night or when alone – Agrimony

■ . . . always on the move – Impatiens

■ . . . caused by anxiety for someone's welfare – Red Chestnut

■ . . . with mood swings and indecisiveness – Scleranthus

■ . . . inability to switch off – Vervain

■ . . . caused by insistent, worrying thoughts – White Chestnut

■ . . . with dissatisfaction over career or life path – Wild Oat

Self-confidence see *Confidence*

Self-pity

■ . . . related to the apparent coldness of friends and family – Chicory

■ . . . related to one's appearance – Crab Apple

■ . . . with talkative over-concentration on one's own life and activities – Heather

■ . . . with resentment or bitterness – Willow

Self-respect see *Inferiority*

Sensitivity

■ . . . to vague fears – Aspen

■ . . . to the way other people do things – Beech, Cerato, Walnut

■ . . . to the possibility of rejection – Chicory

■ . . . to set-backs – Gentian

■ . . . with anxiety, shyness, timidity – Mimulus

■ . . . to possible dangers to loved ones – Red Chestnut

■ . . . to climates of opinion, to change – Walnut

Shock

■ . . . immediate help in a crisis – Rescue Remedy

■ . . . with terror – Rock Rose

■ . . . after-effects of shock, whether recent or a long time ago – Star of Bethlehem

Shyness

■ . . . timidity, etc. – Mimulus

Sleepiness

■ . . . general, or with daydreaming – Clematis

■ . . . at the thought of beginning a task – Hornbeam

■ . . . but still struggling on – Oak

■ . . . after effort or exertion – Olive

■ . . . but mind is still active – Vervain, White Chestnut

■ . . . due to apathy and lack of interest – Wild Rose

Solitude

■ . . . avoided, with preference for parties and good company – Agrimony

■ . . . avoided, with preference for family life – Chicory

■ . . . avoided, with preference for any company – Heather

■ . . . sought out, in order to work faster – Impatiens

■ . . . caused by shyness and fear of social situations – Mimulus

■ . . . sought out in order to enjoy one's own company – Water Violet

Stress

■ . . . dealt with by partying, drinking, drugs – Agrimony

■ . . . due to vague fears – Aspen

■ . . . due to doing too much for others – Centaury

■ . . . leading to loss of self-control – Cherry Plum

■ . . . leading to compulsive behaviour – Crab Apple

■ . . . due to too many responsibilities – Elm

■ . . . self-inflicted by working too fast – Impatiens

■ . . . but still struggling on – Oak

■ . . . leading to exhaustion – Olive

■ ... caused by rigidity and self-denial – Rock Water
■ ... caused by over-enthusiasm and working all hours – Vervain
■ ... due to outside events – Walnut
■ ... with mental arguments, circular thoughts – White Chestnut
■ ... due to lack of clear direction in life – Wild Oat

Strictness

■ ... with other people, with criticism – Beech
■ ... with friends and family, in order to control – Chicory, Vine
■ ... regarding small and unimportant matters – Crab Apple
■ ... with oneself, due to assumed guilt – Pine
■ ... with oneself, in order to live a perfect life – Rock Water
■ ... with others, to make them obey – Vine

Tension

■ ... masked with good humour – Agrimony
■ ... due to intolerance – Beech
■ ... in an effort to stay in control of emotions – Cherry Plum
■ ... due to living in a rush – Impatiens
■ ... because of fear over someone's welfare – Red Chestnut
■ ... due to striving for perfection – Rock Water
■ ... due to indecision – Scleranthus
■ ... because of a shock – Star of Bethlehem
■ ... due to fanaticism – Vervain
■ ... due to inflexibility in ruling others – Vine

Tiredness see *Exhaustion*

Trust (lack of)

■ ... in the abilities of other people – Beech, Impatiens
■ ... in one's judgement – Cerato
■ ... in one's ability to continue coping – Elm
■ ... in the possibility of improvement – Gorse

■ . . . with suspicion – Holly
■ . . . in good things to come – Honeysuckle
■ . . . in one's ability to get started – Hornbeam
■ . . . in one's ability to succeed – Larch

Uncertainty see *Doubt*

Unhappiness see *Depression*

Weakness
■ . . . condemnation of, in others – Beech, Vine
■ . . . with subservience – Centaury
■ . . . regarding rightness of a decision – Cerato
■ . . . of self-control – Cherry Plum
■ . . . faced with a set-back – Gentian
■ . . . faced with a job to do – Hornbeam
■ . . . due to long convalescence, effort – Olive
■ . . . condemnation of, in self – Rock Water
■ . . . with self-pity – Willow

Worry
■ . . . covered over with a laugh – Agrimony
■ . . . due to a vague foreboding – Aspen
■ . . . about rightness of a decision – Cerato
■ . . . over mind giving way – Cherry Plum
■ . . . about other people, in an intrusive way – Chicory
■ . . . over one's appearance – Crab Apple
■ . . . verbalized, over every detail of one's life – Heather
■ . . . due to lack of confidence – Larch
■ . . . due to a known fear – Mimulus
■ . . . over the welfare of someone else – Red Chestnut
■ . . . over which of two or more options to choose – Scleranthus
■ . . . caused by an outside influence or by change – Walnut
■ . . . constant and repetitive – White Chestnut

LEARNING MORE

Further reading

The Twelve Healers and Other Remedies by Dr Edward Bach (The CW Daniel Co, 1936)

Heal Thyself by Dr Edward Bach (The CW Daniel Co, 1931)

The Original Writings of Edward Bach edited by John Ramsell and Judy Howard (The CW Daniel Co, 1990)

The Medical Discoveries of Edward Bach, Physician by Nora Weeks (The CW Daniel Co, 1940)

Bach Flower Remedies: Illustrations and Preparations by Nora Weeks and Victor Bullen (The CW Daniel Co, 1964)

Bach Flower Remedies for Men by Stefan Ball (The CW Daniel Co, 1996)

Bach Flower Remedies for Women by Judy Howard (The CW Daniel Co, 1992)

Growing Up with Bach Flower Remedies by Judy Howard (The CW Daniel Co, 1994)

Bach Flower Remedies for Animals by Stefan Ball and Judy Howard (The CW Daniel Co, 1999)

The Bach Flower Gardener by Stefan Ball (The CW Daniel Co, 1999)

Training courses

You can attend Bach Centre-approved courses in the UK and in many other countries, from New Zealand and the USA to Brazil, Japan and Denmark. Completing all three levels in the Bach International Education Programme entitles you to apply for registration as a practitioner with the Dr Edward Bach Foundation. In addition, many registered practitioners run their own independent courses in the remedies, and an introductory Distance Learning Programme is available. For details of education opportunities near you contact the Bach Centre (see the next section).

USEFUL ADDRESSES

Advice and professional help

For advice on using the remedies and information on education, or to find out where your nearest registered Bach practitioner is, write to:

The Dr Edward Bach Centre
Mount Vernon
Sotwell
Oxon
OX10 0PZ
UK
Tel: 01491 834678
Fax: 01491 825022
www.bachcentre.com
mail@bachcentre.com

Obtaining the remedies

Genuine Bach Flower Remedies carry the 'Bach' signature on the bottle. Distribution around the world is handled by A Nelson & Co. National distributors are appointed from time to time in different countries, and where there is no national distributor Nelsons may export direct. For all information on obtaining remedies contact:

A Nelson & Co
Broadheath House
83 Parkside
London
SW19 5LP
Tel: 020 8780 4200
Fax: 020 8780 5871
www.bachessences.com

Nelson Bach USA
100 Research Drive
Wilmington
MA 01887
Tel: 001 978 988 3833
Fax: 001 508 988 0233
www.nelsonbach.com

INDEX

ty TEACH YOURSELF

ALTERNATIVE MEDICINE

LOULOU BROWN

This practical and safe reference book gives invaluable information on the uses and benefits of both complementary and alternative therapies. With an A–Z of over 50 therapies, and explanations of how to stay healthy with the right therapy, the book provides an essential guide for anyone wanting to find out more about this fast-growing branch of medicine. In addition, a list of conditions and appropriate therapies for treatment of these conditions is included.

From acupuncture, colour therapy and flower remedies to reiki, visualization and yoga, this book gives a well-balanced and comprehensive look at available therapies and how to get the best from them.

Loulou Brown is a writer with a special interest in complementary and alternative medicine. Her first book on the subject, *Working in Complementary and Alternative Medicine*, was published in 1994.

TEACH YOURSELF

REIKI

SANDI LEIR SHUFFREY

Reiki is a popular complementary therapy based on the concept of balancing the energies in the body by meditation and laying-on of hands. This comprehensive guide of Reiki Healing techniques and principles will help to provide a practical solution to suffering and pain resulting in health, vitality, success and enjoyment of living.

- Discover the benefits of self-healing for self-empowerment.
- This comprehensive guide to well-being is suitable for both beginner and more experienced practitioner.
- Explore this practical hands-on, non-invasive technique for healing both friends and family.

One of the few registered Reiki masters in England, Sandi has ten years' professional Reiki experience. She is an extraordinary healer of Spirit.

TEACH YOURSELF

CRYSTAL HEALING

ROGER C. CROXSON

This easy-to-use guide introduces you to the safe and effective use of crystals for healing purposes. From choosing and caring for crystals to administering a healing session, *Teach Yourself Crystal Healing* will help you to get the most out of this remarkable form of complementary healing. This complete course:

- Brings together many aspects of complementary therapies
- Is suitable for both the novice and more experienced worker
- Can be used when working alone or in a group.

Roger C. Croxson is an experienced writer on crystal therapy. He is a practitioner of reflexology, crystal healing, crystal reflexology and shamanism and is founder of the school of crystal reflexology.

Other related titles

TEACH YOURSELF

AROMATHERAPY

DENISE WICHELLO BROWN

What are 'essential oils'? How do they work? How can you use them to improve your health and well-being?

Teach Yourself Aromatherapy provides a comprehensive and highly practical introduction to this increasingly popular complementary therapy. It covers:

- The physical, emotional and spiritual effects of essential oils
- The chemistry of essential oils
- Combining aromatherapy with orthodox medicine
- The various techniques for using the oils
- Detailed information on how to relieve specific medical conditions
- Aromatherapy for pregnancy, childbirth, babies and children.

Denise Wichello Brown is an experienced aromatherapy and massage teacher, practitioner and writer. In this book she gives a complete, no-nonsense reference guide to aromatherapy, suitable for the general reader or for students starting training in aromatherapy, massage or beauty therapy.

Other related titles

TEACH YOURSELF

HOMEOPATHY

GILLIAN STOKES

Homeopathy is a safe and effective complement to conventional medicine for the treatment of humans and animals. *Teach Yourself Homeopathy* offers a clear and simple guide to the principles and methods of this healing art. The book provides a list of remedies suitable for home use in the treatment of minor ailments, together with guidance on how to recognize more serious ones.

This book covers:
- The history and development of homeopathy
- The selection of a remedy
- Self-treatment of common ailments
- Potency and dose
- Consulting professional homeopathic practitioners.

Homeopathy is growing in popularity worldwide and this book provides the essential introduction for all those interested in this form of treatment.

Gillian Stokes is a freelance writer specializing in books on self-help and alternative therapies.